*Wild Mind, Wild Earth*

*Other Books by David Hinton*

# WILD MIND, WILD EARTH

## Our Place in the Sixth Extinction

### DAVID HINTON

SHAMBHALA

Shambhala Publications, Inc.
2129 13th Street
Boulder, Colorado 80302
www.shambhala.com

Cover art: Emperor Hui Tsung (960–1127).
*Auspicious Cranes* (1112), detail.
Liaoning Provincial Museum, Shenyang.
Cover design: Katrina Noble
Interior design: Steve Dyer

9 8 7 6 5 4 3 2

*Printed in the United States of America*

Shambhala Publications makes every effort
to print on acid-free, recycled paper.
Shambhala Publications is distributed worldwide by
Penguin Random House, Inc., and its subsidiaries.

LIBRARY OF CONGRESS CATALOGING-IN-PUBLICATION DATA
Names: Hinton, David, 1954– author.
Title: Wild mind, wild earth: our place in the
sixth extinction / David Hinton.
Description: Boulder: Shambhala, 2022.
Identifiers: LCCN 2022011351 | ISBN 9781645471479 (trade paperback)
Subjects: LCSH: Ecocriticism. | Ecology in literature. | Ecology—
Religious aspects—Buddhism. | Environmental ethics. | Buddhist ethics. |
Buddhism—Environmental aspects. | Global environmental change.
Classification: LCC PN98.E36 H56 2022 | DDC 809/.9336—dc23/eng/20220518
LC record available at https://lccn.loc.gov/2022011351

# Contents

# I

How a Little Poem from
Ancient China Could
Save the Planet

# 1

———————

BEFORE INTENTION and choice, before ideas and understanding and everything we think we know about ourselves—we love this world around us. How can that be? How can we *love* all this when our cultural assumptions tell us in so many ways that we "humans" are fundamentally other than "nature," and that "nature's" only real value is how it supports our well-being? There's no love in that. Doesn't love require kindred natures? And what is kinship with wild earth but wild mind?

How else could we feel exhilarating awe when a majestic orca whale leaps joyfully, yes (forget anthropomorphism, because they are so like us, so kindred) leaps *joyfully* out of the water, twisting spectacularly as it crashes back down: playing, or celebrating, or defiantly shouting *I'm here! I'm me!* to the world, to rivals, to family? And how else could we feel delight at orcas birthing (underwater midwifery!) and nurturing their young? Or feel grief that "southern resident" orcas of the northwest coast are slowly starving to death, anger and guilt that it's because of us: the noise of industrial ship traffic disrupting the echolocation they need to locate prey; polluted seawater; Chinook salmon, their traditional prey, decimated by dammed rivers and overfishing and environmental toxins? We feel despair that because of so much stress those orcas rarely give birth anymore, that the first baby in years died soon after birth and the mother carried it on her nose for seventeen days: above water, hoping it would breathe, hoping it would somehow come back to life. Others sometimes took over the task to let the mother rest, but eventually mother and child both vanished. Heartbreaking. Devastating.

We love this world, this living planet: we feel joy when life thrives, grief when it suffers and dies. This may seem obvious and uninteresting in and of itself. But it's a mystery, isn't it? Because given our Western assumptions, it's inexplicable. Ancient Greek philosophy conjured a transcendental realm of pure idea that seemed more real and true than the empirical world around us—because pure idea is changeless and therefore reliable, while wild earth is constantly changing and therefore unreliable. This transcendental realm was associated with an immortal "soul," establishing a dualism that opens a fundamental rupture between mind and earth. That dualism set the course of Western consciousness—especially as combined with Christian theology—continuing today as an unnoticed cultural assumption that defines the very structure of our everyday experience. And it's quite the opposite of kinship—for it tells us that we are not wild, not earth. It tells us instead that we are the noble "human," in strict opposition to the fundamentally other and lesser "nature."

Togetherness is a primordial value, deeper and more ancient even than self-awareness, let alone philosophizing. It inheres in the body itself. We instinctively need togetherness; and togetherness requires kinship. Indeed, this goes so deep that it challenges our assumptions about individual identity—for without kinship and togetherness, what are we? We curl up together and sink into that primal mystery called sleep. We wake and talk together, cook and eat, make love, and sleep again. We inhabit a single tissue of language (or it inhabits us). We are positively interfused and adrift in it—and in family, community, culture, civilization. And why would it stop with our species?

In the beginnings of human culture, it did not. Amid the first glimmers of human self-consciousness, Paleolithic hunter-gatherers assumed themselves kindred to wild earth, which was itself the "sacred." Though in that cultural context so different from our own, *sacred* couldn't mean anything beyond the mysteriously generative tissue of existence itself. Indeed, in nurturing that kinship, spirituality and art celebrated the wonder of that existence-tissue, its vast and bountiful transformations.

What a deep and unrecognized wound must lay open in us—our Paleolithic kinship with the web of life torn so completely asunder, mind no longer wild and integral to wild earth. That kinship is still there for children today: they instinctively feel it, and they hear it in the stories we tell them, stories full of endearing animal characters. But unlike Paleolithic cultures, our culture strips children of that kinship, leaving us in adulthood bereft of primordial togetherness. It must be an elemental sorrow—to be separated from the wondrous expanse of planetary life, its origins and the forces that drive it. Paleolithic stories tell of that planetary togetherness, speak of creatures like orcas as sisters and brothers, as ancestors. But the foundational stories of our Greek-Christian West describe a self-enclosed human realm separate from everything else. It's a wound so complete we can't see it anymore, for it defines the very nature of what we assume ourselves to be: centers of spirit-identity fundamentally separate from the world around us.

There is an ethics in that wound, for it establishes our human project as the sole center of value. That means "nature" is simply *there for us*—a resource-base for us to exploit however we wish, because it is not human (no reason or soul or language or . . .) and therefore has little intrinsic value. And so, the wound is not only decimating us psychically, however little we are aware of it—it is also decimating earth's ecosystem, ravaging its inhabitants in unimaginable numbers, individual by individual by individual.

But if those assumptions were true about us, how could we love this world? How could we feel so kindred, so emotionally entangled? Entangled through and through—feeling (yes, *feeling!*) the grandeur of mountain peaks towering over deserts or the elegant beauty of a Siberian iris blooming in the garden; savoring chocolate and clementine and espresso; relishing the sun's warmth on our faces, chill clarity of the moon in our eyes. We must be so much more than what we think we are. However deeply we have forgotten it, we must still be wild in our original Paleolithic nature—wild and kindred to wild earth.

That kinship is itself a truly primordial ethics, an ethics before question and argument. For if the ten thousand things of this earth are kindred, their self-realization must have no less value than our own, and harming them must be no less problematic than harming our fellow humans. At bottom, rescuing this planet from its sixth great mass-extinction event is a spiritual/philosophical problem, for it is the unthought assumptions defining us and our relation to the earth that are driving the destruction: the wound that insists we are radically different and qualitatively more valuable than the rest of existence. It's complicated, and we'll get to that. But it's very possible that recognizing and embracing and cultivating our kinship with

6

wild earth is the only thing that might save this planet from its Sixth Extinction, the Great Vanishing now seething through its oceans and continents.

We love this world, and there is an unnoticed philosophical revolution inherent in that love. As we will see, that revolution has been slowly unfolding over the last few centuries in the West, making possible our kindred love for wild earth's ten thousand things. It is a return to Paleolithic understanding (indeed, as we will see, the model of primal cultures helped drive this revolution from its beginning), and that return has a precedent in early China. There, nearly four thousand years ago, a wound very similar to our own defined human consciousness for millennia. But in a vast cultural transformation, it was replaced by the Paleolithic paradigm that had survived beneath the surface of political power structures, a paradigm that revealed our entanglement with existence to be everywhere, all through everything we are. In this alternative paradigm, wild mind kindred to wild earth became the unthought assumption shaping experience— experience, and ethics too.

Perhaps it's too late. Perhaps it's true nothing can save the planet at this point, perhaps the Great Vanishing is already too far along. But this precedent of fundamental cultural transformation in early China makes a similar transformation seem possible here. As our love for this world reveals, this transformation is already quite advanced. Ancient Chinese society was so like ours in its fundamental structures: highly educated and intensely textual, with bureaucratic offices and centralized government, cities, diversified market-economy, sophisticated artistic and intellectual culture, and more. So, ancient China's version of the Paleolithic paradigm could lead the way forward. Sartre said "existence precedes essence,"[1] and he was right. There is no human essence that determines how we can act. Instead, we define that essence always anew in the free choices we make in our day-to-day existence.

We love this world, this living planet—and we also love the stars and galaxies. It's exhilarating to see telescopic images of stars scattered sparkling through space or clustered into swirling galaxies, to learn of their mind-bending lives: the way gravity condenses cosmic dust into stars and ignites them, then finally crushes them into themselves so violently that they explode and seed space with the rich dust that will become a new generation of stars and planets like ours. Our kinship seems to know no bounds! And in rediscovering that kinship, how can we help but discover vast and beautiful dimensions of ourselves that had been lost: human consciousness woven profoundly through the planetary ecosystem, woven indeed through the entire Cosmos?

Yes, we are much more than what we think we are, and that is liberation of astounding proportions. Even simple perception: a gaze into star-strewn night skies, for instance, or streamwater braiding liquid light between stones. In sight, we find that utter belonging quite literally and scientifically true. The Cosmos evolved countless suns and planets; and here on our planet Earth, it evolved life-forms with image-forming eyes like ours. So what else is that gaze but the very Cosmos looking out at itself? What is thinking but the Cosmos contemplating itself? And our inexplicable love for this world, our delight and grief— what is that but the Cosmos loving itself, delighting in itself, grieving for itself? We are wild through and through: wild mind, wild earth, wild Cosmos. This is how Paleolithic and ancient Chinese people[2] understood it. And it seems clear enough, even self-evident, once we step outside the cultural assumptions we have inherited.

This is our most magisterial identity, an identity that encompasses all of existence: the ten thousand things of earth and

Cosmos looking out through our eyes. In their expansive and ravishing dimensions we find our kinship with those things, our love and emotional entanglement. And we also find an ethics, for what happens to earth quite literally happens to us. Who knew ethics could be so beautiful, this valuing of the ten thousand things each in its own exquisite and individual clarity? Here it is, that ethics distilled into a simple-seeming little poem of crystalline seeing that was written by Tu Mu in ninth-century China:

### Egrets

Robes of snow, crests of snow, and beaks of azure jade,
they fish in shadowy streams. Then startling away into

flight, they leave emerald mountains for lit distances.
Pear blossoms, a tree-full, tumble in the evening wind.

# 2

In his critique of the West's human-centered perspective, Robinson Jeffers proposes a radical philosophical vision:

I believe that the universe is one being, all its parts are different expressions of the same energy, and they are all in communication with each other, influencing each other, therefore parts of one organic whole. (This is physics, I believe, as well as religion.) The parts change and pass, or die, people and races and rocks and stars, none of them seems to me important in itself, but only the whole. This whole is in all its parts so beautiful, and is felt by me to be so intensely in earnest, that I am compelled to love it, and to think of it as divine. It seems to me that this whole alone is worthy of the deeper sort of love; and that here is peace, freedom, I might say a kind of salvation, in turning one's affection outward toward this one God, rather than inward on one's self, or on humanity, or on human imagination and abstractions...[3]

America's seminal landscape poet writing early in the twentieth century, in a stone house set atop granite cliffs on the California coastline, Jeffers operated outside of the West's human-centered perspective. Indeed, although there are hints of that radical perspective in earlier writers like Alexander von Humboldt, Henry David Thoreau, and John Muir—Jeffers may be the first writer in the West to wholly adopt it, together with its challenging implications. And he proposed shifting our source of value from the human to the organic whole of earth and Cosmos, which he described as "one being":

> ... Integrity is wholeness, the greatest beauty is
> Organic wholeness, the wholeness of life and things, the
>     divine beauty of
>         the universe. Love that, not man [*sic*]
> Apart from that ... [4]

Jeffers was caught at the terminological limit of Christianity and the pantheism of his Romantic forebears (p. 37 ff.), still depending on divinity to explain his experience of a Cosmos so wondrous. But the reality he is actually describing is quite different: the Cosmos as a single living "organic whole" whose most fundamental nature is change and transformation, and in which the human plays no special role. If he had encountered ancient Chinese thought, he might have recognized this universe as Tao (道: "Way"): the name Lao Tzu (c. fifth-sixth centuries B.C.E.) used for the Cosmos conceived as a single living tissue, "one being" that he conceived as generative, as "female" and "mother." This Tao is reality in and of itself magisterial and awe-inspiring: a generative cosmological process, an ontological pathWay by which earth's "ten thousand things" appear and disappear in an ongoing process of transformation: each emerging into existence, evolving through its life, and then going out of existence, only to be transformed and reemerge in a new form. And in this cosmology, humans are just one among these ten thousand things.

Jeffers proposes that we reintegrate our minds with this organic whole:

> We must uncenter our minds from ourselves;
> We must unhumanize our views a little, and become
> confident
> As the rock and ocean that we were made from.[5]

This is clearly a challenging task. Challenging, but also profoundly liberating, for it opens our self-enclosed alienation to new possibilities of dwelling as integral to "rock and ocean," earth and its processes. Jeffers offers no actual method to do that, but it is the whole purpose of Taoist and Ch'an (Zen) Buddhist spiritual practice in ancient China: to integrate consciousness with this Tao, this "one being," to heal that vast wound of consciousness torn from wild earth. It is the most fundamental question for Ch'an practice, and perhaps for human consciousness in general, especially in this time of the Sixth Extinction's Great Vanishing: how to move past the illusory separation between consciousness and Cosmos, which entails erasing the seeming separation between subjective and objective, mind and landscape, Self and Cosmos. We might today call this a deep-ecological practice—for it is the cultivation of our original wild nature, our lost kinship with the web of life, a kinship that necessarily invests the web of life with ethical value. This was the assumption among Paleolithic hunter-gatherers, and the basis for Buddhism's foundational ethical principle of *ahimsa* (Chinese 不害: "no harm"): in compassion, to avoid all unnecessary harm.

Ch'an was not a religious project: it was an empirically based spiritual/philosophical one. At the center of Taoist-Ch'an practice was meditation, which is essentially observational science turned inward. Meditation reveals the basic contours of wild mind, and cultivates a return to wild mind belonging to wild earth. In its barest philosophical outlines, meditation begins with sitting quietly and watching thoughts come and go in a field of silent and dark emptiness. From this attention to thought's movement comes meditation's first revelation: that we are, as a matter of observable fact, separate from our thoughts and memories. That is, we are not the center of identity (the West's "soul") we assume ourselves to be in our day-to-day lives—that center of self-absorbed thought that takes empirical reality as the object of its contemplation, defining us as fundamentally outside reality. Instead, we are wild: the empty awareness (known in Ch'an terminology as "empty-mind") that watches identity rehearsing itself in thoughts and memories relentlessly coming and going.

With experience, the thought process slows, and it is possible to watch thoughts burgeon forth out of the dark emptiness, evolve through their transformations, and disappear back into that emptiness. Thoughts, it seems, appear and disappear in exactly the same way as the ten thousand things of the empirical Cosmos appear and disappear—and so, thought and things share as their primal source the same generative emptiness. In this, meditation reveals that our mental processes too are wild by their very nature—always already integral to the living tissue of a generative Cosmos.

Eventually the stream of thought falls silent, and we inhabit empty-mind, that generative ground itself. Here, we are wholly free of the identity-center—free, that is, of the self-absorbed and relentless process of thought that defines us as centers of identity separate from the world around us. This is the heart of Ch'an dwelling: mind and Cosmos woven together in the most profound cosmological and ontological way, identity revealed in its most capacious and primal form as nothing less than the generative tissue itself, the gentle and nurturing "mother."

By now it's clear that meditation is itself a radical ecological practice—even if only practiced enough to see the basic structures it reveals, structures of wild mind integral to wild earth. It is a remarkably simple and direct way to heal that wound of consciousness torn from the tissue of existence. And in that healing, things begin to look different. Once mind is empty and silent, perception becomes a particularly spiritual form of ecological practice: awareness, the opening of consciousness, functions as a mirror reflecting the world with perfect clarity, allowing no distinction between inside and outside. Hence, the ten thousand things become the very content of consciousness, become indeed identity itself. This empty-mind mirroring is a celebration of absolute kinship—consciousness become the Cosmos gazing out at itself. And so, deep seeing too is a practice that heals the wound of consciousness.

Empty-mind mirroring reintegrates consciousness and wild earth's ten thousand things as a matter of everyday immediate experience. This everyday attention to the sheer thusness of things—whether it is gazing at streamwater braiding light through rocks or traffic weaving through city streets—is therefore a deep-ecological practice. It is a celebration, and it is an ethics—for in honoring the elemental thusness of things in and of themselves, it asserts for them a value both elemental and absolute. And so, Ch'an practice is the cultivation of love at primordial levels, for to see things this deeply is to love them. It is to see as the Cosmos—and yet, how strange: the Cosmos is perfectly indifferent, but through us it loves the ten thousand things of this world.

That love is the fabric of classical Chinese poetry, which cultivates kinship with the world by rendering landscape (literally "rivers-and-mountains") in concise images. Its imagistic clarity manifests that Ch'an empty-mind mirroring—earth's vast rivers-and-mountains landscape replacing thought and even identity itself, revealing the unity of consciousness and landscape/earth/Cosmos. It thereby renders a larger identity, an expansive identity made quite literally of wild-earth landscape and its ten thousand things. Here, the ethics of deep seeing and thusness is invested with new depths: what is done to wild earth is done to us, as Mencius (fourth century B.C.E.) affirmed early in the development of ancient China's conceptual framework when he said "the ten thousand things are all there in me. And there is no joy greater than looking within and finding myself faithful to them."[6] And so, Tu Mu's vast little poem is an ethics:

### Egrets

Robes of snow, crests of snow, and beaks of azure jade,
they fish in shadowy streams. Then startling away into

flight, they leave emerald mountains for lit distances.
Pear blossoms, a tree-full, tumble in the evening wind.

# 3

Robinson Jeffers's poems inevitably address, one way or another, the wound of modern consciousness and its ethical consequences, clearly delineated in a fuller version of the passage we saw earlier (p. 12):

> A severed hand
> Is an ugly thing, and man [sic] dissevered from the earth
> and stars and his history
> ... for contemplation or in fact ...
> Often appears atrociously ugly. Integrity is wholeness, the
> greatest beauty is
> Organic wholeness, the wholeness of life and things, the
> divine beauty of
> the universe. Love that, not man [sic]
> Apart from that, or else you will share man's pitiful confusions,
> or drown in despair when his days darken.

Jeffers advocates for kinship at an elemental level—indeed, he speaks out of that kinship. His is an elemental voice of the planet itself, a poetry of long booming lines moving with the cadences of Pacific surf pounding against the continent's edge below his home on the California coast, as in these lines from his magisterial "Continent's End" (1924), where he addresses the sea as our "mother":

### Continent's End

At the equinox when the earth was veiled in a late rain,
    wreathed with wet poppies, waiting spring,
The ocean swelled for a far storm and beat its boundary, the
    ground-swell shook the beds of granite.

I gazing at the boundaries of granite and spray, the
    established sea-marks, felt behind me
Mountain and plain, the immense breadth of the continent,
    before me the mass and doubled stretch of water.

I said: You yoke the Aleutian seal-rocks with the lava and
    coral sowings that flower the south,
Over your flood the life that sought the sunrise faces ours
    that has followed the evening star.

The long migrations meet across you and it is nothing to you,
    you have forgotten us, mother.
You were much younger when we crawled out of the womb
    and lay in the sun's eye on the tideline.

It was long and long ago; we have grown proud since then
    and you have grown bitter; life retains
Your mobile soft unquiet strength; and envies hardness, the
    insolent quietness of stone.

The tides are in our veins, we still mirror the stars, life is your
    child, but there is in me

Older and harder than life and more impartial, the eye that
   watched before there was an ocean.

That watched you fill your beds out of the condensation of
   thin vapor and watched you change them,
That saw you soft and violent wear your boundaries down,
   eat rock, shift places with the continents.

Mother, though my song's measure is like your surf-beat's
   ancient rhythm I never learned it of you.
Before there was any water there were tides of fire, both our
   tones flow from the older fountain.

However unlikely it may seem, Jeffers's imposing poems are
close kin to "Egrets." "Egrets" seems effortless, operating at ease
within an ecocentric philosophical tradition—but for Jeffers, it
was quite different. As his ecocentric perspective is a fundamen-
tal challenge to the human-centered Western tradition, he can't
avoid a stern polemic of radical ethical intent—for even now, a
century later, his idea that the self-realization of wild earth
and its individual inhabitants is just as valuable as human self-
realization remains altogether foreign, if not reprehensible, even
to most environmentalists. And it didn't help that Jeffers taunt-
ingly called his ideas "inhumanism," which he defined as "a shift-
ing of emphasis and significance from man [sic] to not-man; the
rejection of human solipsism and recognition of the trans-human
magnificence."[7] Jeffers speaks for planet and Cosmos, decrying
the environmental impact of a human population grown too large
and self-involved and rapacious. But at the same time, Jeffers is
proposing a revolutionary (for the West) form of self-realization,
a liberating self-transformation in which we reestablish our wild-
mind kinship with that "organic wholeness" of the wild earth and
Cosmos. And because we haven't done that, he imagines

The earth, in her childlike prophetic sleep,
Keeps dreaming of the bath of a storm that prepares up
    the long coast
Of the future to scour more than her sea-lines:
The cities gone down, the people fewer and the hawks
    more numerous,
The rivers mouth to source pure; when the two-footed
Mammal, being someways one of the nobler animals, regains
The dignity of room, the value of rareness.[8]

Jeffers forged his insights a century ago. Since then, it has become increasingly clear how accurate his evaluation was. Human population and destructive exploitation have increased exponentially—and as a result, we are currently in the midst of a Great Vanishing that will in all likelihood include the human race. It turns out, as Jeffers predicted, the "storm that prepares up the long coast / Of the future" has arrived, and it is the human animal itself.

———

About half a century after Jeffers sounded the alarm, as the terrifying dimensions of earth's Sixth Extinction were beginning to be recognized, the historian Lynn White wrote a seminal and widely influential essay, "The Historical Roots of Our Ecological Crisis" (1967). In it, White found the human-centered perspective that Jeffers challenged was, quite simply, the Christian paradigm, its creation myth setting the stage for widespread ecological destruction:

By gradual stages a loving and all-powerful God had created light and darkness, the heavenly bodies, the earth and all its plants, animals, birds, and fishes. Finally, God had created

Adam and, as an afterthought, Eve to keep man from being lonely. Man named all the animals, thus establishing his dominance over them. God planned all of this explicitly for man's benefit and rule: no item in the physical creation had any purpose save to serve man's purposes. And, although man's body is made of clay, he is not simply part of nature: he is made in God's image.

. . . Christianity is the most anthropocentric religion the world has seen. . . . Man shares, in great measure, God's transcendence of nature. Christianity, in absolute contrast to ancient paganism and Asia's religions (except, perhaps, Zoroastrianism), not only established a dualism of man and nature but also insisted that it is God's will that man exploit nature for his proper ends.[9]

This story places us above the rest of "creation" and makes our exploitation of the earth a divine imperative—for in God's broader intent, we humans inhabit earth as part of a divine plan of redemption. We are being tested, and earth is the proving ground, intended for our use as we prove our worthiness to rejoin God and enjoy eternal bliss in heaven. Wild landscape was nothing more than a stage and resource-base for the human adventure—something to dominate, possess, and exploit on the journey to spiritual realms more real than this earthly one. It is a bizarre and fantastical scheme, and the results have been catastrophic.

Perhaps it's true nothing can save the planet at this point, perhaps the Great Vanishing is already too far along. Functioning as a barely noticed body of assumptions, that Greek-Christian paradigm has conjured every aspect of our material lives—the whole self-involved globalized consumer-driven capitalist extravaganza, which accords little or no value to the non-human.

Perhaps it's too late to change that, and it's all too abstract now, too distant. Who would personally slaughter a newborn orca for a few gallons of gasoline? But we keep putting gasoline in our cars, and faraway oil tankers keep plowing through the orca's waters, and that baby orca dies.

It is the very nature of our material existence that needs to change. The only way that will happen, White proposes, is with a wholesale transformation in the cultural assumptions shaping our material existenc-e. The Chinese word for those cultural assumptions is 經, built from the basic element "silk": 糸, which in its early more clearly pictographic form was 帛, showing a pair of cocoons with silk emerging in the form of three strands that would have been spun into thread. 經 originally meant the "warp" upon which cross-threads are woven to create patterned cloth. It came to mean the enduring elements upon which the patterns of culture and consciousness are woven, hence: "the classics," or "a culture's abiding concepts or principles." That is, structures that articulate and preserve cultural assumptions that define our lifeways: philosophy, literature, art.

To overthrow the cultural assumptions that shape our thinking and experience: that would be to open ourselves wholly to wild-mind kinship and love, but it cannot be an easy thing. Those unthought assumptions represent our philosophical home, our orientation in the world, our very identity—and leaving the assurance and comfort of home is always difficult. The Greek-Christian paradigm is still widely influential in our society. And it is late, very late. But as we will soon see, a paradigm shift is already well underway here, a cultural transformation that began with the discovery of another ancient poem—Lucretius's *On the Nature of Things*—and continuing through the Scientific Revolution in the seventeenth century, then the pantheistic philosophers and poets of the eighteenth and nineteenth centuries.

And again, it has happened before. There is a precedent: ancient China, where three thousand years ago the culture underwent a monumental cultural transformation that was essentially the same as the one already underway here, the one our planet needs so badly. The early graph for "cultural warp-threads" is 經, in which the silk element is augmented with those for water (川: pictographic image of a river's rippling current) and earth (土, stylized version of 凸, the early oracle-bone form showing a lump of clay on a potter's wheel). And so, as we will see in the next chapter, the cultural warp-threads created by that ancient Chinese transformation were earth and water: the planet itself.

# 4

ALL OVER THE WORLD, Paleolithic hunter-gatherers lived integral to wild earth—in small bands, their shelters fleeting, wandering landscape and living off the bounty of fecund earth. Paleolithic art and ritual and spirituality celebrated wild earth, its lavish generative power, and our belonging to its wondrous transformations. But with the Neolithic revolution—occurring across a staggered timeline in different areas, but starting about ten to fifteen thousand years ago (later in North America, where skepticism about its advantageousness meant that it was only adopted indecisively in a few areas before the European invasion, and often abandoned in preference for hunter-gatherer lifeways)—people began settling into villages, permanent enclaves separate from the landscape, a separation exponentially intensified in our modern urban culture. And there, they began controlling "nature" in the form of domesticated plants and animals, thereby inscribing into their daily lives a detached instrumentalist relationship to the world. And along with this, wild earth came to be seen not as kindred, but as a threat to the cultivated human realm, as something that must be overcome to increase safety and productivity.

This revolution was reflected in a spiritual revolution. Neolithic cultures adopted otherworldly deities who had that same relation to wild earth: outside and detached and controlling. These were anthropocentric religions, in which religious practice was about convincing those deities to control reality for the benefit of humankind. This culminated in Judeo-Christian monotheism and the world's other "great" religions—the lone exception being Buddhism. In China, this transformation was complete by the Shang (1766–1040 B.C.E.), China's first historical dynasty. Shang culture was built on a spiritualized monotheistic paradigm hardly different in its fundamental outlines from the Christian West. In the Shang, it was believed that all things were created and controlled by an all-powerful monotheistic deity very like the sky-god of Christian theology, a deity known simply as Lord-Celestial (上帝: Shang-Ti). And as in the traditional West, people experienced themselves as spirits who would return in death to inhabit Lord-Celestial's spirit realm.

The Shang rulers held power because in the cultural myth they were descendants of Lord-Celestial, and through prayer and sacrifice they could influence how he directed the flow of events. But eventually, those rulers grew unbearably tyrannical, and the dynasty was overthrown. It was replaced by the Chou Dynasty (1040–223 B.C.E.), whose rulers reinvented Lord-Celestial as an impersonal "Heaven," thus ending the Shang's claim to legitimacy by lineage. The Chou rulers justified their rule by claiming they had the "Mandate of Heaven," so when their rule began to falter, the last semblance of theocratic cosmology crumbled, leaving no organizing system to structure society.

The "Hundred Schools" of thought, including philosophers like Lao Tzu and Confucius (c. fifth-sixth centuries B.C.E.), struggled to invent a new philosophical framework that could replace the spiritualistic system with a humanistic one based on empirical reality. One transitional aspect of this transformation was the reinvention of Heaven as an entirely empirical concept: the generative cosmological force that drives the perennial change of earth's natural process. It was a strategy to secularize the sacred while at the same time investing the secular with sacred dimensions, and we will see it replicated twenty-five hundred years later in the West, when conventional Christianity is replaced among the intellectual class by various forms of pantheism.

This transitional concept of Heaven was replaced in Lao Tzu's thought by the entirely secular concept that we have already encountered (p. 12): Tao, which was essentially synonymous with Heaven, but without Heaven's metaphysical dimension. This Tao was at the heart of a cultural framework growing out of the Paleolithic worldview that had survived beneath the Shang's theocratic power structure. Here, the human was again assumed to be woven into earth and Cosmos, human intelligence (mind/spirit) understood as a wholly natural phenomenon, part of a cosmic "intelligence." This was not theology, suggesting we partake of some divine intelligence behind the Cosmos. And it was not anthropomorphism, attributing human attributes to the Cosmos. Instead, it recognized what science leaves unnoticed in its explanations of reality: the bedrock mystery that our Cosmos has an inherent capacity to order and organize itself (exactly what science studies and deciphers). And isn't that what "intelligence" is at an elemental level—the capacity to order and organize? For the ancient Chinese, human intelligence was just one particular instance of that more general organizing capacity of the Cosmos.

There is in classical Chinese a name for this: 意, which has a range of meanings: "intentionality," "desire," "meaning," "insight," "thought," "intelligence," "mind" (the faculty of thought). The natural Western assumption would be that these traits refer uniquely to human consciousness, but 意 is also often used philosophically in relation to the non-human world. In this usage, it means the "intentionality/desire/intelligence," the inherent ordering capacity, that shapes reality's ongoing cosmological process of change and transformation. Each particular thing, at its very origin, has its own 意, as does the Cosmos as a whole.

This range of meaning links our human mind (intention/thought) to the generative movements of the Cosmos, describing human thought as just one manifestation of an "intelligence" that infuses all existence. 意 is therefore a capacity that human thought shares with wild animals and landscape and indeed the entire Cosmos—a reflection of the Chinese assumption that the human and non-human form a single tissue that "thinks" and "wants." In this, mind is not a transcendental identity-center separate from and looking out on reality, as we assume in the West. It is instead woven wholly into the ever-generative tissue of a living and "intelligent" Cosmos.

As an extension of the breach between human consciousness and "nature," Western culture assumes human civilization is radically different from "nature," a metaphysical dualism that recapitulates the separation of heaven and earth, subject and object, language and reality, etc. It's there in the meaning of the word *nature*, which excludes humankind and its civilizations from wild earth by definition, and so reveals that dualism as an unnoticed cultural assumption. As with the West's other metaphysical dualisms, this divide between human civilization and "nature" was unknown in primal cultures, where there simply was no "civilized" space in contradistinction to "natural" space—whether mental or physical. And it was also unknown in ancient China, even though China did very much have the distinct "civilized" space of a complex urban civilization.

China's integration of "civilization" and "nature" is summarized in the ideogram 文, which refers to the patterns of the Cosmos, patterns created by 意. Those patterns include such things as veins in stone and ripples in water, the patterns of stars and seasonal progressions, life and death, the diverse array of the ten thousand things and their transformations, and finally, as another of those "natural" patterns, civilization: cities and markets, government and philosophy, poetry and painting. Indeed, 文 is the base-element for a broad range of ideograms having to do with writing, literature, and culture. And it seems obvious, of course, once we forget the arbitrary metaphysical structures of the Greek-Christian West: given that *Homo sapiens* is indisputably just one among countless life-forms that have appeared through the planet's evolutionary processes, how could even complex symphony orchestras or particle accelerators be anything other than "nature"? When we see our human endeavor this way, as itself wild, we can see ourselves as integral to wild earth. And from this understanding comes an ethical assumption according to which we act from love and kinship for the entire tissue of life.

# 5

FLEEING LOS ANGELES in 1914, Robinson Jeffers and his new wife discovered the wild beauty of the Carmel / Big Sur coastline and felt they had come home to their "inevitable place." Jeffers was the originary American landscape poet, and it was his immersion in this breathtaking landscape that liberated him from our human-centered perspective. And why not? As the ancient Chinese knew so well, wild landscape is where we can know as immediate experience the non-human on its own vast scale, where we can sense the magisterial dimensions of wild earth, feel like a small and integral part of its "organic wholeness." And the intent of Jeffers's poetry is similar to that of ancient Chinese rivers-and-mountains poems like "Egrets": to make us feel things from that perspective of ecocentric belonging.

Europe's human-centered assumptions historically precluded this kind of landscape experience, this integration of human and landscape. The Greek-Christian framework hid us from our original-nature as integral to the planetary ecosystem, and therefore kindred to all life. In that sense, it has denied our humanity in the most fundamental way. A homeland that is beautiful and spiritual, sustaining and transforming—such attitudes toward wild landscape are familiar today, but they were all but unknown in the West until a few centuries ago. More typical was William Bradford, looking out from the decks of the *Mayflower* when it arrived off Cape Cod in 1620, describing wild North America in his journal as "a hideous and desolate wilderness, full of wild beasts and wild men."[10] *Wild* in the Christian framework: a term of derision and disgust. Indeed, it was considered evil, needing to be tamed and civilized, harmonized with God's divine order.

But by Bradford's time, a cultural transformation very similar to ancient China's had begun to take shape in the West, and it would fundamentally change our relation to wild earth. Just as we look to a poem from an ancient culture for new insight, that cultural transformation began with a poem recovered from another lost classical culture: Lucretius's *On the Nature of Things* (c. 75 B.C.E.), an epic philosophical poem from the Roman Empire that developed ideas of the ancient Greek philosopher Epicurus (341–270 B.C.E.). Epicurus stood in explicit opposition to Platonism, whose spiritualized metaphysics established a dichotomy between a transcendental "soul" and "nature," a metaphysics that supported Christian theology and defined the assumptions that shaped experience in the West. Through persecution and the burning of books and libraries, Christianity had erased as heretical virtually all of the Greek and Roman intellectual heritage, especially the Epicurean school of thought to which Lucretius belonged. *On the Nature of Things* had been lost for fifteen hundred years, before a copy was discovered in 1417 hiding in the shadows of a monastic library in the mountains of Germany. Slowly, over the next few centuries, the radical ideas in *On the Nature of Things* almost singlehandedly launched the Scientific Revolution and the Enlightenment: again, the ancient as the most radically new.

Remarkably congruent with Taoist thought in early China, Lucretius's radical ideas represented a resurgence of Paleolithic materialism, its immediacy and kinship with wild earth. He described nature as a generative mother, and the fundamental nature of things as change: a constant process of creation, destruction, and regeneration. He saw how humans belong wholly to this Cosmos, how we are only a small part of its vast and wondrous processes, consciousness/soul made of the same stuff as everything else. For Lucretius, there is no human meaning to things, no end or purpose toward which things progress. He thought that we humans are kindred to the other animals, which possess interior lives very like our own, and that this kinship necessitates a sympathy and moral responsibility to them. Finally, he rejected any notion of a God who creates or controls reality according to whims and miracles—proposing instead that there is a natural explanation for everything. As part of this materialist approach, he thought the Cosmos is ordered by inherent natural laws that can be understood through observation and reason. And from all of this, he derived a deep joy and wonder at the Cosmos, its vast splendor and our utter kinship to that splendor.

The Scientific Revolution slowly worked out the implications of Lucretius's poem, implicitly valuing the ten thousand things in and of themselves: the empirical and physical rather than mythological and metaphysical. This shift in allegiance helped give rise to an influential animal-rights movement. And more generally, it slowly revealed the full dimensions of our kinship, progressively pushing humans from the center of "creation," revealing how we are a small and integral part of a vast Cosmos: Copernicus proving that Earth is not the center of the universe, Darwin that the human is integral to the animal

kingdom (an idea anticipated in Lucretius, along with evolu-
tion), Lyell that Earth has a geologic life of its own that predates
humanity by vast stretches of time, Freud that the ego (soul) is
not the center of identity, Hubble that the universe stretches
out beyond us across inconceivable distances of space con-
taining countless galaxies like our own, and that it is expand-
ing at unbelievable speeds.

But at the same time, science also precluded a sense of funda-
mental kinship because it fiercely objectifies "nature," thereby
intensifying the Greek-Christian separation of mind/soul
and "nature." It saw "nature" as a mechanistic assemblage of
facts that are the object of *analysis* (a violent act of "breaking
something complex into simple elements," from the proto-Indo-
European *leu*: "to divide, cut apart") and knowledge, a resource
from which data is mined—another form of that detached and
instrumentalist relation to "nature." It was uninterested in in-
vesting empirical reality with a compelling poetic or spiritual
vision. That fell to the poets and thinkers of the time, who were
also fundamentally influenced by Lucretius's poem and the sen-
sibility it engendered. The British Romantics were the vanguard
here; and remarkably, they were no less influenced by Native
American cultures.

Beginning in the early seventeenth century and reinforcing
the revolutionary ideas in Lucretius's poem, accounts began to
appear in print describing Native American lifeways, and they
became widely influential as a critique of Europe's cultural
assumptions—the Christian paradigm, which was indeed the
only known possibility in Europe at the time. This "indigenous
critique" includes most importantly for us that sense of human
kinship with the wild, but it also included a broad range of ideas
that challenged European assumptions, and which combined
with Lucretius's poem to become a crucial catalyst for Europe's

Enlightenment: reason and empirical argument, individual freedom, social equality (including notably for women).[11] This widely read, even popular, literature included reports describing sage Indian elders, their native wisdom and critiques of European civilization and its philosophical assumptions, as well as many descriptions of native cultures by missionaries and travelers in North America. These books inspired, to take one highly influential example, Rousseau's claims that primitive societies afforded people richer and more satisfying lives than the "civilizations" of Europe. Although such books were generally dismissed in conventional circles for their admiring portrayal of supposedly "savage" native people in North America—they were broadly read and highly influential among intellectuals, offering for the first time in European culture a real vision of human and nature that was radically different from the Christian narrative (and they would later be no less influential for Thoreau and his intellectual compatriots in nineteenth-century America).

Attentive to the possibilities suggested by accounts of Native Americans living in harmony with "nature," the British Romantic poets were discovering in mountain landscape and wild nature a rapturous experience that felt sublime and spiritual, even transcendent. This is primordial human kinship with wild earth reemerging into consciousness with great intensity. With it came the West's first inklings of wild mind. The shock of possibility offered by the "indigenous critique" was pivotal for William Wordsworth around 1798, the moment when his thought took the distinctive radical turn we find in poems like "Lines Composed a Few Miles above Tintern Abbey" (see pp. 37–38). He envisioned his ideal life in England's Lake District on the model of sage Native Americans living in harmony and communion with unspoiled nature, which for him meant body and spirit liberated into an intense physical immediacy.

Imagining childhood in his epic poem *The Preludes*—to take one simple and direct example—Wordsworth described himself as a young Native American suffused in this communion, a richness later stolen from him by the urban alienation of "civilization," with its industrialization and commercialism:

> Oh! many a time have I, a five years' Child,
> A naked Boy, in one delightful Rill,
> A little Mill-race sever'd from his stream,
> Made one long bathing of a summer's day.
> Bask'd in the sun, and plunged, and bask'd again
> Alternate all a summer's day, or cours'd
> Over the sandy fields, leaping through groves
> Of yellow grunsel, or when crag and hill,
> The woods, and distant Skiddaw's lofty height,
> Were bronz'd with a deep radiance, stood alone
> Beneath the sky, as if I had been born
> On Indian Plains, and from my Mother's hut
> Had run abroad in wantonness, to sport,
> A naked Savage, in the thunder shower.[12]

Wordsworth and the Romantics were profoundly influential among American intellectuals—and through this influence, that new embrace of wild mind and wild earth was soon passed back to America, opening Thoreau and later figures to the more wholesale and transformational influence of Native American culture that still survived all around them. Thoreau's seclusion at Walden Pond was a practice of self-cultivation meant to approximate—as much as realistically possible given his own cultural situation—the Indian way of life, to take only one of countless examples for this seminal figure who made a lifetime study of Native American culture, both from books and direct contact.

But however influential, the full philosophical dimensions of primal culture were, to what little extent they were understood, a step too far. Wordsworth and his compatriots still needed to conceive their revolution within the as-yet-unimpeachable Christian framework—and in that framework, the only explanation for those rapturous feelings was some kind of communion with a divine presence in landscape. In this, the world was invested with a sense of sacred wonder. It was a process that exactly paralleled the transitional pantheism we saw in China three millennia earlier (p. 27), when Heaven was redefined as "the natural processes of wild earth."

This was the pantheism of Baruch Spinoza in the seventeenth century ("The more we know of particular things, the more we know of God," he declared in *The Ethics* of 1677); and of Deism, the prevailing conceptual framework among America's eighteenth-century intellectuals (including the founding fathers). But more important for us are the British Romantic poets and the Transcendentalism of Emerson and Thoreau— for there, pantheism begins to take the form of personal/spiritual self-realization, as in Samuel Taylor Coleridge's "Frost at Midnight" and William Wordsworth's "Lines Composed a Few Miles above Tintern Abbey," epochal poems written by close friends in 1798, at the beginning of the Romantic tradition:

> . . . wander like a breeze
> By lakes and sandy shores, beneath the crags
> Of ancient mountain, and beneath the clouds,
> Which image in their bulk both lakes and shores
> And mountain crags: so shalt thou see and hear
> The lovely shapes and sounds intelligible
> Of that eternal language, which thy God
> Utters, who from eternity doth teach

Himself in all, and all things in himself.
Great universal Teacher! ... (*Coleridge*)


                ... And I have felt
A presence that disturbs me with the joy
Of elevated thoughts; a sense sublime
Of something far more deeply interfused,
Whose dwelling is the light of setting suns,
And the round ocean and the living air,
And the blue sky, and in the mind of man:
A motion and a spirit, that impels
All thinking things, all objects of all thought,
And rolls through all things. Therefore am I still
A lover of the meadows and the woods
And mountains; and of all that we behold
From this green earth; of all the mighty world ...
                I, so long
A worshipper of Nature, hither came
Unwearied in that service ... (*Wordsworth*)


Pantheism was a compelling vision—beautiful, poetic, spiritual, cosmic. And because it valued "nature," it dramatically opened the possibility of loving kinship. But still, at the fundamental structural level, it leaves the Christian separation of human and "nature" intact—for sacred nature remains "out there," divine. We remain human, struggling spiritually and artistically to connect with that divine. Kinship remains a distant and detached relationship, and it was never a relationship with earth in and of itself. There is no wild mind integral to wild earth. Meanwhile, as the strict empiricism of science increasingly came to define our assumptions about the world, the idea of a divine presence in the Cosmos became more and more unconvincing, whether it was a conventional Christian god in the heavens or a pantheistic divinity of earthly nature itself.

The profoundly spiritual response of Romantic poets to nature came directly from the immediate experience of it as infused with the wondrous and sublime, which they could only conceptualize as divinity. But as that divinity became intellectually untenable, the wondrous and sublime remained. Scientist and nature-writer Alexander von Humboldt (1769–1859) was among the first to recognize and explore the possibilities this new clarity opened (new and old: Lucretius again, and the indigenous model). Humboldt was an international superstar—a notable influence on Wordsworth and Coleridge (confirming and expanding the radical approach they had developed), and positively transformative for the American line of environmental thinkers: Emerson, Thoreau, Whitman, and on to Muir and Jeffers.[13] His hugely influential writing dispensed with God or the divine, and proposed that our awe in the face of sublime wilderness derives from our "communion with nature" as a magisterial presence, "a unity in diversity of phenomena; a harmony, blending together all created things, however dissimilar in form and attributes; one great whole animated by the breath of life." Here he means *breath* not in the sense of some divine agency, but as a single unifying life-force inherent to the material Cosmos, for he elsewhere describes the Cosmos as "animated by one breath" and "animated by internal forces." In sharp contrast to the scientific description of nature as a kind of machine, Humboldt recognized earth as an organic whole, a living web of interrelated life: a "net-like intricate fabric," a "wonderful web of organic life."

As Romanticism evolved in America from Emerson and Thoreau through Whitman and Muir toward Jeffers—Humboldt's secular vision, its challenge to the need for divinity, haunted their thought, appearing at the most radical moments in their writing. It was a vision of wild mind in relation to wild earth beginning to resemble the Paleolithic and Taoist-Ch'an paradigms. Here, wild earth itself, without recourse to dimensions of divinity, is the open door to spiritual self-transformation and realization: visionary and transporting, as in the cosmology shaping Tu Mu's Taoist-Ch'an egret poem. Or Thoreau's *Journals*, to take one example from the West's process of cultural transformation. Perhaps the most radical work of the nineteenth century, the *Journals* record an intense and daily mirror-deep attention to the actual immediate world, valuing and celebrating its miraculous presence as sufficient and even ravishing in its every detail. Hence, a practice of deep Ch'an insight.

The West's grand cultural transformation continued into the twentieth century. Existentialism and phenomenology tried to move past the West's spiritualized thinking to a direct engagement with our immediate *existence*. Science, of course, continued relentless in that engagement. Here in America, extending the possibilities opened by Humboldt and Thoreau and Muir, there was a proliferation of nature writing, some quite popular and having a broad impact in the culture: from John Burroughs to Rachel Carson and beyond.

And innovative twentieth-century American poetry included perhaps the most radical challenge to the West's anthropocentric framework. It begins with Ezra Pound early in the century, who borrowed from ancient China the imagism of Tu Mu's egret poem and its Ch'an assumptions about empty-mind mirroring. Images became the fabric of modern poetry, and Pound described their effect in a decidedly Ch'an way as "the precise instant when a thing outward and objective transforms itself, or darts into a thing inward and subjective,"[14] a principle William

Carlos Williams soon restated as "no ideas but in things."[15] In mid-century, Charles Olson deepened this eco-poetic impulse when he described the function of poetry as

> the getting rid of the lyrical interference of the individual as ego, of the "subject" and his [sic] soul, that peculiar presumption by which western man [sic] has interposed himself between what he is as a creature of nature (with certain instructions to carry out) and those other creations of nature . . .

For Olson, a poem is spontaneous and improvisational, driven by the oral rhythms of the body, the breath. In other words, it moves with the energy of the Cosmos, moves indeed from the generative source of existence and its actions. He proclaims that a

> poet will [go] down through the workings of his [sic] own throat to that place where breath comes from, where breath has its beginnings, where drama has to come from, where, the coincidence is, all act springs.[16]

And so, throughout the century, innovative American poetry has functioned as a philosophical project intent on liberating us from the alienated Western Self; returning us to our original animal nature; and reintegrating us at the deepest levels of consciousness with landscape and ecosystem, earth and Cosmos.[17] Though they can hardly suggest the range of this poetry's strategies, these two short poems were written mid-century by the major heirs to Jeffers's poetry of California landscape, Kenneth Rexroth and Gary Snyder, who were both writing in the Sierra Nevada mountains, where America's environmental movement began when John Muir helped found the Sierra Club in 1892 (here, Rexroth followed by Snyder):

## The Lights in the Sky Are Stars

Lying under the stars,
In the summer night,
Late, while the autumn
Constellations climb the sky,
As the Cluster of Hercules
Falls down the west
I put the telescope by
And watch Deneb
Move towards the zenith.
My body is asleep. Only
My eyes and brain are awake.
The stars stand around me
Like gold eyes. I can no longer
Tell where I begin and leave off.
The faint breeze in the dark pines,
And the invisible grass,
The tipping earth, the swarming stars
Have an eye that sees itself.


## Wave

Grooving clam shell
    streakt through marble,
   sweeping down ponderosa pine bark-scale
    rip-cut tree grain
            sand-dunes, lava
              flow

Wave        wife.
        woman—wyfman—
"veiled;   vibrating;   vague"

sawtooth ranges pulsing;
    veins on the back of the hand.

Forkt out: birdsfoot-alluvium
   wash

   great dunes rolling
Each inch rippld, every grain a wave.

Leaning against sand cornices til they blow away

  —wind, shake
stiff thorns of cholla, ocotillo
sometimes I get stuck in thickets—

Ah, trembling spreading radiating wyf
    racing zebra
 catch me and fling me wide
To the dancing grain of things
     of my mind!

Not surprisingly, given Western culture's rigorously human-centered assumptions, wild-earth landscape did not become a major subject of painting until the nineteenth century. Europe's Romantic painters and America's Hudson River School (p. 44) portrayed landscape with much the same sublime majesty as that found in Romantic poets like Wordsworth, or here in Percy Bysshe Shelley's "Mont Blanc" (1816), where the mountain's grandeur puts Shelley in "a trance sublime and strange," a state evoked in tempestuous descriptions of the magisterial mountain "wilderness":

  . . . the very spirit fails,
Driven like a homeless cloud from steep to steep

Albert Bierstadt: *Among the Sierra Nevada*, California (1868). Smithsonian American Art Museum

That vanishes among the viewless gales!
Far, far above, piercing the infinite sky,
Mont Blanc appears—still, snowy, and serene;
Its subject mountains their unearthly forms
Pile around it, ice and rock; broad vales between
Of frozen floods, unfathomable deeps,
Blue as the overhanging heaven, that spread
And wind among the accumulated steeps;
A desert peopled by the storms alone,
Save when the eagle brings some hunter's bone,
And the wolf tracks her there—how hideously
Its shapes are heap'd around! rude, bare, and high,
Ghastly, and scarr'd, and riven. . . .

Impressionist and post-Impressionist painters took a more "secularized" approach to landscape. But they were no less enthralled with its beauty and form, its inherent life and energy, making their paintings implicit acts of kinship.

The interest in landscape faded in twentieth-century visual arts (with a number of influential exceptions like late Monet and Cézanne, Georgia O'Keefe, Milton Avery, Ansel Adams). But challenging the hegemony of our rational mind/soul, liberating us from its constraints, was surely the primary engine of artistic innovation across the twentieth century. We find it manifest in a host of radical strategies: primitivism, surrealism, Dada, abstraction, gestural (wild!) abstraction, chance operations, minimalism. And finally, Land Art began in the late 1960s making art from nature itself, or art in which the artist is replaced by nature's own processes—thereby integrating human and nature, and dispensing in powerful ways with the human-centered framework.

Meanwhile, as the influence of that Romantic celebration of nature spread through the culture, people began aspiring to spend time in natural settings. This led to extensive systems of national and state parks and preserves. As wealth and leisure and the automobile made people more mobile, those parks and preserves became standard vacation destinations for urban and suburban Americans. Now, over three hundred million people visit the National Park system alone—and this firsthand experience with wild earth could only foster feelings of love and kinship. (It's worth remembering, though, that the National Forest Service and the Department of the Interior, which oversee America's public lands, value wild land primarily as a resource to exploit, whether through extraction or tourism.)

Nevertheless, a major contributor to our contemporary environmental crisis is the simple fact that so much of the human race inhabits cities and has little or no direct contact with wild earth, so how could they value it? Nature films and television shows address this, and may in fact be the most broadly influential advocates for wild earth in our culture at large. They portray animals and ecosystems with remarkable and endearing intimacy—animals very often living in their own cultural contexts and on their own terms. Here we see their innate intelligence, emotional world, social connections, etc.—all of which inspire a recognition of both our kinship with them and their own self-worth, thereby suggesting a sense of human belonging to planetary ecosystems.

But even if it has brought widespread environmental advocacy, the West's philosophical transformation remains ungrounded. Our sense of kinship still lacks the profound depths of Taoist-Ch'an ontology/cosmology. Still, that cultural transformation has come to the verge of Taoist-Ch'an understanding, which is why the ancient Chinese precedent seems so relevant at this moment—especially because its philosophical depths are empirically based, and therefore not only well-suited to our scientific paradigm, but already implicit in it.

It may seem too obvious to state, but it's important to note another striking parallel between the cultural transformations in ancient China and the modern West. From the British Romantics through contemporary American poets and Land Artists, it is the same as for ancient China's Taoist-Ch'an thought and practice and art: in both traditions, cultivating and exploring our immediate experience of the world around us is the most essential and profound method of self-cultivation and self-realization. It is the way to understand one's deepest nature in its most expansive form: wild mind integral to wild earth. And as it turns out, this cultivation of wholeness for self is, miraculously, also cultivation of wholeness for the planet.

# 6

WITHIN THE WEST'S epochal cultural transformation, Jeffers held a crucial place. Although caught in the terminological limitations bequeathed him by his pantheistic forebears, he was a radical step beyond them. His vision was fundamentally post-Christian, for it was not at all human-centered. He valued wild earth in and of itself, for its own self-realization—not for how it can benefit or inspire humanity. And from this came Jeffers's earth-based ethics—that we should love the whole, not the human alone—an ethics that led him to say "I'd sooner, except the penalties, kill a man than a hawk."[18]

Aldo Leopold's widely influential "land ethic" (from his essay "The Land Ethic" in *The Sand County Almanac*, 1949) proposes a philosophical principle consonant with Jeffers's spiritual vision, locating primary ethical value in ecosystem and earth:

> The land ethic simply enlarges the boundaries of the [ethical] community to include soils, waters, plants, and animals, or collectively: the land . . .

In short, a land ethic changes the role of *Homo sapiens* from conqueror of the land-community to plain member and citizen of it. It implies respect for his [*sic*] fellow-members, and also respect for the community as such ...

... Obligations have no meaning without conscience, and the problem we face is the extension of social conscience from people to land.

These principles led Leopold to a concise ethical imperative: "A thing is right when it tends to preserve the integrity, stability, and beauty of the biotic community. It is wrong when it tends otherwise." This is, of course, wild mind acting as integral to wild earth.

Born in the same year as Jeffers, Leopold had an influential career in the Forest Service and as an academic, during which he furthered John Muir's political work arguing for the value of wilderness. And indeed, his land ethic became a principal theoretical support for the vision of conservation that defines mainstream environmentalism today: stewardship, the idea that humans should be "stewards" who care for and preserve the "natural" world. (Leopold and Muir were quite successful as political advocates, as it turns out, key voices in convincing the government to establish conservation policies such as national parks and wilderness areas.) Stewardship is a step beyond traditional Western assumptions, to be sure, but it inevitably reverts to human-centered values and to the benefits preserved landscape offers us humans: scenery, recreation, spiritual sustenance, scientific data, habitable environment. These are all essentially instrumental and exploitative. Stewardship generally operates within the Christian paradigm that still commands the allegiance of a broad swath of the population and their political leaders. And so, on the one hand, it has brought considerable practical success. But on the other hand, it remains intensely contested by conservative elements who share the Christian paradigm and still believe earth and its ten thousand things are simply *there for us*. And because the two sides share the same paradigm, there is no way to move past the argument, no way to fundamentally change our relation to wild earth. The effectiveness of stewardship will therefore remain limited, and we will continue down the path we are on.

Given the staggering technological power we have acquired, stewardship is humanity's *de facto* relationship to earth at this point. To work, stewardship needs to be based on the non-anthropocentric assumption of fundamental kinship between human and non-human, an assumption that must exist before question and argument, shaping experience and action: the vision, as we have begun to see, of Paleolithic and ancient Chinese cultures. Only that will allow us to value earth and its individual life-forms in and of themselves, to value their own self-realization as we do our own. Leopold recognized this. Anticipating Lynn White by two decades, Leopold spoke of the need for a paradigm shift to support his land ethic, admitting that

> no important change in ethics was ever accomplished without an internal change in our intellectual emphasis, loyalties, affections, and convictions. The proof that conservation has not yet touched these foundations of conduct lies in the fact that philosophy and religion have not yet heard of it.

Here, Leopold is recognizing the foundational role played by the "warp-threads" (經) upon which a culture is woven. He made no attempt to imagine a new paradigm, a new system of "warp-threads." He seemed unaware that such a paradigm was already coming into view as a result of the cultural transformation we have traced, and he surely didn't suspect its full dimensions in the Paleolithic/Chinese paradigm to which we will return. In any case, this alternative paradigm was certainly not broadly influential in the society, and its absence has continued to haunt mainstream environmentalism, leaving it without spiritual/philosophical "loyalties, affections, and convictions" that could ground its aspirations in a coherent way. Without such a paradigm shift, it's unlikely even our own self-interest will change behavior much, because the impact of our actions is so remote and abstract that we rarely feel it in any immediate way. The absence of an ecocentric paradigm haunts not only the large environmental organizations, which remain generally anthropocentric in their stewardship advocacy, but also mainstream environmental writing.

In his widely influential book *The End of Nature* (1989), Bill McKibben returns repeatedly to a need for the kind of radical paradigm shifts proposed by Romantic pantheism and Robinson Jeffers, Eastern spirituality and deep ecology—alternately raising and dismissing them as unrealistic given our cultural situation and therefore not worth exploring in any detail. He may very well be right, but it's a lacuna that undermines his hope that scientific arguments will be enough to change the unfolding catastrophe—because so long as we operate in the West's human-centered framework, the science describing eco-devastation alone is unlikely to change human behavior in substantial ways. This so haunts his argument that it resurfaces as the very last words of his book. After speaking of the patterns we imagine in the stars as an example of the patterns through which humans order and control "nature," he ends, sounding for all the world like the Jeffers he has already dismissed as "vague, transcendental": "we will need to train ourselves not to see those patterns. The comfort we need is inhuman." This is wild mind integral to wild earth, seeing as the Cosmos sees, the vision Rexroth comes to at the end of "The Lights in the Sky Are Stars" (p. 42):

The tipping earth, the swarming stars
Have an eye that sees itself.

# 7

SOON AFTER Leopold's land ethic appeared, that ecocentric paradigm that the West had "not yet heard of" came more into view among intellectuals during America's cultural revolution of the fifties and sixties. There was a powerful philosophical dimension driving their rejection of the otherworldly and puritanical (*no* to the body, the physical, the earth!) Christianity that had dominated American society. Jeffers was an admired elder for these cultural revolutionaries, largely because he proposed a transformation from anthropocentric to ecocentric, an earth-based challenge to the West's human-centered culture. Their ecocentric passions led most dramatically to a form of environmental advocacy quite different from and more philosophically coherent than the stewardship model of mainstream environmental groups: the direct action of radical eco-warriors like Greenpeace and EarthFirst!, who described themselves as earth defending itself.

Many of those postwar intellectuals also recognized that ecocentric view in primal (especially local Native American, a reprise of the British Romantics, Thoreau, etc.) and Asian cultures, where it was indeed the very terms of spirituality. In this, the seminal Gary Snyder (pp. 41–43) was perhaps the most original and influential voice. Snyder was a serious student of both Ch'an and primal cultures. One crucial dimension in his broad-ranging thought is the ecological wisdom in Ch'an's cultivation of wild-earth thusness through immediate empty-mind experience. He augments this with the primitive, where "people live vastly in the present." And to the wholeness of primal and Ch'an wisdom, he contrasts the wound of Western consciousness, warning that

a culture that alienates itself from the very ground of its own being—from wilderness outside (that is to say, wild nature, the wild, self-contained, self-informing ecosystems) and from that other wilderness, the wilderness within—is doomed to a very destructive behavior, ultimately perhaps self-destructive behavior.[19]

In fact, as we have begun to see, Paleolithic assumptions defined the Taoist-Ch'an conceptual framework of ancient Chinese culture. According to those assumptions, the human was integral to earth and its ten thousand things—and so, people belonged wholly to earth's natural processes. Indeed, the concept of "nature" or "wild"—everything outside the human realm—would be inconceivable for Paleolithic hunter-gatherers because they had no human cultural space distinct from wild earth, no subjective realm distinct from the objective, and therefore no separation between human and non-human.

The hunter-gatherers who originally inhabited North America, for instance, knew no fundamental distinction between themselves and the animals they hunted. They recognized that the animal world had an interior life kindred to humans. There was no human-centered assumption that we humans are qualitatively more valuable, as in the Western tradition. And from this follows an ethics: to hunt only out of real necessity, and never in a frivolous or disrespectful way. Accordingly, these people hunted with humility and prayer and sacrifice to the hunted animal, for they considered animals their sisters or brothers. Or perhaps ancestors. Or perhaps still more accurately, past/future forms of themselves. And yet: not them*selves*, not any *selves*. For there was no concept of selfhood in any sense we would normally recognize, selfhood that we unwittingly project when we try to translate or anthropologically imagine ourselves into such cultures.

The hunted animal dies so the hunter can live; and next time, it will be the hunter's turn to die so that the other can live. This is a profound sense of interspecies and intergenerational love, this offering of oneself so another can continue to live. And more: because there was no distinction between self/spirit and body, to eat another animal was to eat its entire being, not just its body: like their flesh, indeed indistinguishable from their flesh, their identity and nature became part of you. This is a stunningly clear and revealing account of reality: profound, beautiful, accurate, and so challenging to our own assumptions that it's difficult even to quite comprehend, for it changes everything.

Here is a world infused throughout with "spirit," a term mistakenly used by anthropologists trying to imagine themselves into primal cultures, but never really leaving their own. For the concept in primal cultures was nothing like our Western "spirit" or "soul." Instead, it was fluid and permeable through different life-forms, a universal life-force breathing through things—which is an understanding that survived into the ancient Chinese paradigm, in concepts such as *ch'i* (氣). *Ch'i* is often translated as "life-force" or "breath-force." But there is no dualism here, as our conceptual framework automatically assumes, no separation of reality into matter and a "breath-force" ("spirit") that infuses it with life. Rather, *ch'i* is both breath-force and matter simultaneously. Hence, the Cosmos as a single tissue dynamic and generative through and through, matter and energy a single breath-force surging through its perpetual transformations—a vision remarkably like Humboldt's "one great whole animated by the breath of life" (p. 39).

This generative ontology/cosmology is nothing like ours. For us, linear time operates as a completely unnoticed assumption about the nature of reality, a grand metaphysical structure we take for granted. Without realizing, we inhabit that metaphysical dimension, another radical separation of the human and wild earth itself. This metaphysics of time operates in the structure of our language, and accordingly shapes consciousness at unthought foundational levels. It's there in the inflected grammar, verbs conjugated to place everything within the temporal dimensions of past, present, future. And it's there in the structure of written language, which (largely because of its functional limitations) moves in a straight line, sentences beginning and progressing to an end, one sentence leading to the next, one thought leading to the next. But thought itself, in preliterate primal cultures and even now (however much our assumptions blind us to the fact), is itself more spatial and cyclical and impermanent, just as spoken language is: wandering and vanishing, fragmenting and branching, moving somewhere new and then returning to earlier thoughts, thoughts then reshaped and soon themselves vanishing. It moves as empirical reality moves.

There is no reason to think this dimension we call "time" exists. If we look for it, we find nothing—nothing beyond change itself, wild earth's ongoing process of transformation. And that is how primal and ancient Chinese cultures experience it: not as a linear progression, but as an ongoing and all-encompassing generative moment. In his "An American Indian Model of the Universe" (1936, published 1950/56), Benjamin Whorf recognized this same ontology/cosmology in the Hopi language, which at the deep levels of grammar retains Paleolithic structures. He describes the Hopi sense that reality is "manifest" from a potentiality that

> exists in the mind, or as the Hopi would prefer to say, in the heart, not only the heart of man [sic], but in the heart of animals, plants, and things, and behind and within all the forms and appearances of nature in the heart of nature, and by an implication and extension which has been felt by more than one anthropologist, yet would hardly ever be spoken of by a Hopi himself [sic], so charged is the idea with religious and magical awesomeness, in the very heart of the Cosmos, itself.[20]

This process of emergence from "the very heart of the Cosmos itself" survives in the Chinese concept of *ch'i*, and also *tzu-jan*: literally meaning "self-so" or "the of-itself," emphasizing the particularity and self-sufficiency, the *thusness*, of each of the ten thousand things (mental and physical) that make up the generative process of Tao. And it survives, as in the Hopi, at the foundational level of language itself: rather than verb tenses inscribing linear time into consciousness, classical Chinese simply registers emergence, *tzu-jan*, occurrence appearing of itself in a kind of boundless present. And so, as an unthought assumption: Tao, reality seen as a generative tissue—as female, mother.

Ethics, spirituality, cosmology: it's all embodied in the arts, which do indeed bring a culture's "warp-threads" (Leopold's "intellectual emphasis, loyalties, affections, and convictions") to life for its people. And at this point in history, it's hard to avoid the conclusion that if art or literature isn't about wild mind, about grounding it in wild earth, it is beside the point or part of the problem. For they are just more human self-involvement reinforcing the detached human realm that stands in hostile or indifferent relation to earth. Indeed, from the absolute perspective of wild earth/Cosmos, aren't they in a profound way quite meaningless because they are stripped from their true context, and so have no frame of reference within which to take on real meaning?

In the Paleolithic, poems and stories told of human existence integral to landscape and other animals (what we call "animals"—for like the spirit-body and subject-object dualisms, this human-animal dichotomy was unknown to hunter-gatherers). And visual art portrayed primarily the non-human animal world: cave-art in prehistoric Europe, for instance, or petroglyphs here in North America. Humans often appear in this art, but rendered as belonging to the animal world, to the ecosystem's fabric of life. Cave art was inscribed into spaces that felt like birthing-chambers of earth's living reality. And petroglyphs are etched out in landscape itself, becoming part of landscape.

This stands in stark contrast to European art, for its "intellectual emphasis, loyalties, affections, and convictions" were quite the opposite. In Europe, as we have seen, wild earth only became a late and short-lived interest in the form of landscape painting. But Paleolithic art, whatever else it expresses, inherently celebrates people's place as integral to a vast web of living being. And because that Paleolithic kinship remains our original-nature, because the West's philosophical transformation has begun to reveal that long-hidden original-nature—we respond to it this way today, feel its celebration of kinship.

As White and Leopold would recognize, these profoundly

different conceptual paradigms entail altogether different ethics—and accordingly, different environmental impacts. The instrumentalist exploitation made possible by an alien spirit-center was quite simply inconceivable for Paleolithic hunter-gatherers. Wherever Europeans went, they found primal cultures woven into intact ecosystems. But armed with Greek-Christian philosophical assumptions that enable an instrumental relation to earth, they quickly ravaged those landscapes and their indigenous cultures. Native Americans had inhabited North America for fifteen thousand years (and those southern resident orcas their home territory for seven hundred thousand years)—still, the ecosystem was basically whole and balanced and vital. It was quite the opposite with Christian Europeans, however: within a few decades of their arrival anywhere on the continent, they decimated the landscape and nearly everything that lived there, individual by individual by individual.

Paleolithic art expresses (to apply Leopold's principle) an ethics that inheres in a system of spirituality and cosmology: reality as a single living tissue in which identity ("spirit") is fluid and permeable through different life-forms. It is a spirituality/cosmology everywhere evident in primal culture. Evident not just in art, but also in ritual and hunting practices, and in the way coastal tribes considered orcas their ancestors—not merely in some mythic sense, as it might appear from outside, but quite literally. And even today, with all the overlays of Western culture, if a southwest Indian hears with particular clarity a nearby bird's wingbeat, she might say: "See, there, the ancestors are always with us!"

# 8

Lynn White identifies the Christian story of divinely sanctioned human dominance and exploitation as the "root of our ecological crisis," but the more fundamental way Christian mythology facilitates environmental destruction is its bedrock ontological/cosmological structure. This structure, reinforcing ancient Greek philosophy, divides the Cosmos into two ontologically distinct regions: the spirit realm (heaven and soul), and the material realm (earth and body). As we have seen, it's a cosmology that conceives the human as a spirit that lives on earth as a kind of alien come from a distant spirit-place, with no fundamental connection to material earth, and therefore no kinship with earth's ten thousand things. Ethically, this reduces earth to a mere resource-base having no intrinsic value.

However, the spirit-center Self is a creature of cultural structures that precede Greek and Christian thought by millennia. Indeed, those conditions were necessary preconditions for the Christian paradigm, which gave that spirit-self mythic dimensions (as did the world's other major religious paradigms, excluding Buddhism). Leopold and White recognize that a radical paradigm shift is needed to stop environmental destruction—even if they didn't quite see, as Jeffers did, that it needs to be a fundamentally non-human-centered vision, a vision in which the well-being of the ecosystem is the primary value and bedrock assumption. As we have seen, that paradigm shift has been taking shape over the last few centuries in the West, but it has struggled against much more than its advocates knew.

The Christian paradigm is only the surface—and even though it has been broadly replaced in our culture by the various dimensions of secular humanism, that kind of change won't accomplish much unless we recognize and learn to see through the underlying structures that made the Christian paradigm possible. At the heart of those structures is the spirit-center self, and radical transformation needs to begin there, because the conditions that gave rise to the transcendental spirit continue to support that structure even now in our post-Christian age, where religious belief in an eternal soul is hardly the unquestioned assumption.

As we have seen, Paleolithic hunter-gatherers assumed that the human was wholly integral to earth and its ten thousand things. There was no isolate identity-center, no sense of the human as fundamentally different than or separate from "nature." Remarkable and unlikely as it may sound, they were in crucial ways closer to our orca cousins than they are to us, for both had an organic sense of identity integral to earth's processes (which is not at all to say they didn't have individuality and reason, imagination, social organization, and all the rest: they did; but then, so do those orca cousins, in their own particular ways). The Paleolithic community of kinship/identity extended beyond the human to include the ecosystem and its creatures.

Indeed, they might say something like "we *are* the land," or "we know this land through the minds of animals." And that sense of identity generated an ethics that valued everything in the web of life, not just the human.

As we have seen, the spirit-center grew out of a rupture between Self and world that began decisively when agrarian Neolithic cultures replaced the Paleolithic. People began settling into villages, permanent enclaves separate from the landscape, and controlling "nature" in the form of domesticated plants and animals. This was an altogether new relation to wild earth, which thereby became not only other, but also something to be overcome, domesticated. In this, Neolithic people's lives were structured as a detached instrumentalist relationship to the world—the beginning of our sense that the world is simply *there for us.*

Not long after the Neolithic revolution came writing— another act of human domination over the world, conceptually bringing it under one's control, possessing it. Writing completed the rupture, creating the illusion of a permanent and immaterial identity-center. In preliterate cultures, language existed only as thought and speech, which move in the same generative way everything else moves: appearing, evolving, disappearing, always to be replaced by new forms. They certainly possessed powerful mental abilities (reason, imagination, etc.), but did not experience mental content as permanent, as existing differently than things in the empirical realm. Instead, thought/language moved the way anything else moved: days and nights, weather and seasons, streamwater and wind, etc. Hence, primal people experienced no fundamental difference between subjective and objective processes (one of the primary realizations meditation offers). It is quite remarkable to imagine: the world of knowledge in preliterate cultures extended only as far as the memory of individuals and their community. But with writing, people could inscribe thoughts, making them seem permanent. They could come back to those thoughts later, reenter and relive and revise them, and others could read those thoughts in distant times and places. Writing seems to defy the fleeting nature of our inner reality, creating the illusion of an immaterial and timeless subjective world, a mental realm of permanence that is separate from the ever-changing world in a way so fundamental it can only be described as ontological. Hence, the illusion of language (coincidental with the "soul") as an inner realm looking out on the outer realm of empirical reality.

Further reifying this transcendental identity-center ("soul") alien to earth, words representing the world evolved from pictographic immediacy to alphabetic script, wherein they have an arbitrary and symbolic relationship to the world of things, reinforcing this separation of subjectivity and the world. Words seem to point at those things as if from some kind of outside. This intensified the illusion of language and thought as a transcendental realm looking out on earth's ten thousand things as an ontologically separate realm, objects out there and other than us. This separation haunts modern environmental thinking, although it is rarely recognized. One momentary exception occurs in Elizabeth Kolbert's celebrated *The Sixth Extinction* (2014). Near the end of her book, Kolbert mentions without further comment how foundational structures predating the dominant Western paradigm undermine our entire utilitarian science-based understanding of the dire situation and its possible remedies. These are the ineluctable structures that conjured our detached, instrumental, and exploitative relation to earth: "As soon as humans started using signs and symbols to represent the natural world, they pushed beyond the limits of that world." It is an admission that the situation is likely beyond remedy.

This immaterial subjective realm created by alphabetic writing is the illusory spirit-center soul reified in Greek philosophy and Christian theology. In fact, those systems can be described as the philosophical discovery and exploration of that seemingly changeless internal realm that Neolithic lifeways and written language had recently conjured. And the same can generally be said about the world's other great religions (with the exception, again, of Buddhism). Enthralled by subjectivity's seemingly transcendental reaches, they created mythologies around it. For the ancient Greeks, it was a "soul" identified with reason, which participated in the realm of "forms": reason's changeless ideas that are considered more real and true than the always changeable empirical world. This "soul" was associated with the sacred, and it was eventually incorporated into Christian theology/cosmology, where it became transcendental and kindred to an otherworldly sky-god. And further: it was divinely enshrined as the very raison d'etre of the entire universe.

The subjective/objective dualism engineered by this illusory spirit-center even defines our experience of perception itself: creating the illusion that it is a kind of inside looking out on an outside, thereby making the breach between mind and earth the very texture of moment-to-moment experience. But looking closely at what happens in the actual moment of perception— we find no self, no subject and object, no inside and outside. What we find instead is simply consciousness open to the world, consciousness like a mirror filled with the world: another of the realizations Ch'an meditation offers. In other words: the Cosmos looking out at itself. Again, the "I" appears only after the fact. Because our stories tell us that we are identity-centers, we say "I look," "I see," etc. And this fact is reified in the very structure of our language as an unrecognized but foundational assumption, for our grammar requires a subject for those verbs:

that "I" whose importance cannot be overstated, and to which we will return later, for it is absent in classical Chinese. (Notice that when a breaching orca's celebration is described on p. 3 as expressing *I'm here! I'm me!*, our language projects a Greek-Christian spirit-center into the orca. Orca identity is obviously quite different—and yet, it's the only grammatical way we can say it.)

Etymology too reveals the illusory nature of our seemingly transcendental Self. If we search the archaeology of mind, trace the etymologies of words describing mental states and processes back toward their origins, we find that they all came into the mental realm from the empirical. That is, they originally referred to images from the observable universe—things or processes or physical behavior. The human mind slowly created the "transcendental Self" from those images through a complex process of metaphoric transference, thereby weaving the structures of identity from the empirical Cosmos. On its way back into the primal word-hoard, *consider* can be traced to the Latin root-elements *con* ("with") + *sîdus* ("star/constellation"), to take but one example. And *ponder* can be traced to the fragrant and colorful bustle of a marketplace in the Latin *penderâre*, meaning "to weigh."

The end result of these "soul-building" processes was a foundational separation of human and "nature." And as for "nature": the end result of alphabetic writing and Greek-Christian dualism was a radical devaluation of the material world. It had, first, no language, and so no meaning; then, no inherent rational order, and so no inner reality; and finally, no spirit, and so no transcendental value. This devaluation continues for us as an operant assumption at a more fundamental level than the Christian story that White identifies as the "root of our ecological crisis." That story still shapes the unthought assumptions of many in our society, those for whom Christian belief remains vital—but even for those who live in a post-Christian intellectual world, this spiritualized Self remains fundamentally unchanged. In fact, the wound that spiritualized Self opens makes everything instrumental and exploitative. For us, now, even when we appreciate landscape/nature, we are not integral to it. It is not part of us, not kindred. It is instead commodity: data, scenery, perhaps spiritual sustenance. And even our environmental concerns themselves are instrumental and exploitative: for they are primarily driven not by an interest in wild earth's inherent value, but by a desire to sustain our human interests.

White argues that the Christian paradigm has led to our current ecological crisis. And it's a huge part of the story. But the source of that depredation is most fundamentally the transcendental spirit-center that predates and gave rise to our anthropocentric Greek-Christian paradigm, to the fundamental breach between human and everything else.

Quite aside from the Christian story, this detached relation defines modern science, with its rigorous objectivity: the defining intellectual disposition of our era. Science too is instrumental, treating the world as a resource-base to be mined for data, or as a kind of machine it can cut up ("analyze") and understand, opening the way for technology's manipulation and exploitation. This critique was widespread during the postwar revolution in thinking, and was described in extensive philosophical and historical detail by Carolyn Merchant in her widely influential *The Death of Nature: Women, Ecology, and the Scientific Revolution* (1980). There, Merchant shows how the Scientific Revolution completed the dismantling of that organicist vision of earth as a Great Mother, a vision that enforced ethical constraints on human actions, replacing it with a vision of nature as a dead mechanism without inherent value and therefore available for unlimited exploitation.

And in terms of modern political structures, that detached Self is the bedrock assumption shaping neoliberal capitalism, with its unregulated and unrestrained economic activity and growth that takes individual and human profit as its ultimate values. This too finds its roots in the Neolithic, which brought the beginning of wealth in the form of land ownership and storable goods—and with that came class distinctions and inequality and social injustice, not to mention that elemental and environmentally devastating force, greed. Science/technology and capitalism are obviously extremely effective evolutionary strategies for our species. At the same time, they are remarkably effective forces of ecological devastation. Empowered by science/technology and capitalism, the illusory spirit-self enables ruthlessly efficient exploitation of the world from a wholly detached perspective, and it has led us to the brink of ecological collapse.

But, as we are beginning to see in the alternative Paleolithic and Chinese paradigms, the West's "soul" and its cosmology are not at all accurate or self-evident descriptions of reality. They are conjurings that appeared through the vicissitudes of human evolution, becoming entrenched because they gave the species a stunning selective advantage. They exist as the defining structures of modern *Homo sapiens* consciousness, and the function of Ch'an practice is to unravel those structures, revealing our original-nature prior to those structures. It is now all too clear that the selective advantage of the Neolithic/writing spirit-center is over. Now that detached spirit-center is the engine destroying our species, and it seems selective advantage has shifted to the Paleolithic/Chinese paradigm of wild mind integral to wild earth.

# 9

THE RADICAL RETHINKING of conceptual paradigms in the cultural revolution of the sixties was well-advanced when Lynn White wrote "The Historical Roots of Our Ecological Crisis" in 1967—and Ch'an (Zen) Buddhism was an integral part of that revolution. White recognized the culture was still broadly under the sway of Christian assumptions, so he thought it more realistic to propose an ecologically benevolent form of Christianity: St. Francis's quasi-pantheistic vision of love and care for earth and its creatures, essentially the conventional steward-ship model. One saint cannot undo the entire Christian edifice, though. And like Bill McKibben, who was haunted by more radical alternatives while recognizing that social realities seemed to make them unfeasible, White with uncanny clarity recognized Zen Buddhism as the radical and thoroughgoing paradigm-shift:

The beatniks, who are the basic revolutionaries of our time, show a sound instinct in their affinity for Zen Buddhism, which conceives of the man-nature relationship as very nearly the mirror image [i.e. "opposite"] of the Christian view.

There is much to learn from the Paleolithic paradigm. Of course, ethics now cannot be as direct and immediate as it was among hunter-gatherers. It can only be indirect and abstract, our actions having distant ecological impacts, and prescriptions must involve complex social policy and direction. And in any case, that paradigm seems impossibly distant—for material culture structures consciousness, and our material culture is completely different from that of Paleolithic hunter-gatherers. We do not live in constant and intimate contact with earth's weave of life. We do not wander landscapes with handmade tools, hunting and gathering. And we are irremediably post-Neolithic, shaped absolutely by the Neolithic's instrumentalist human-nature divide.

But as we have begun to see, the Paleolithic survived into ancient Chinese culture, where it was refashioned to form the Taoist-Ch'an conceptual framework: White's "beatnik" Zen (Ch'an was adopted from China by Japan, where it was known by the Japanese pronunciation of the *ch'an* ideogram: "Zen"). And in fact, Taoism-Ch'an shaped thought in a society structured very much like our own. Like us, ancient Chinese scholar-officials were highly educated, empirically minded, and intensely textual. They worked in offices as government bureaucrats. They produced a complex body of cultural work: philosophy, poetry, painting, calligraphy. They inhabited large and internationally cosmopolitan cities, and traveled widely between those cities and also deep into rural and wilderness areas. All of this within a highly diversified economy with the same basic elements as ours: money, markets, agriculture, artisans, merchants, transportation, etc. Thus, unlike the Paleolithic model, the Taoist-Ch'an framework seems to offer a more directly applicable alternative to the Western paradigm—a way of opening ourselves to our original wild-mind nature, its elemental kinship with wild earth, and the ecocentric ethics implicit in that transformation. And indeed, it seems to be a fully formed articulation of the conceptual framework emerging from the cultural transformation that has unfolded over the last few centuries in the West—and which was, like Taoism-Ch'an, inspired from its beginning by the philosophical insights of Paleolithic cultures.

In the Taoist-Ch'an paradigm, as we have seen, humankind belongs to the Cosmos conceived as a living and self-generating tissue. Ch'an meditation opens us to empty-mind, revealing our original nature prior to the rupture that emerged from Neolithic lifeways and alphabetic writing. And empty-mind's mirror-deep seeing also returns us to immediate experience prior to that rupture, for it reveals wild earth's ten thousand things as part of us. Hence, Ch'an as a deep-ecological practice in which we see through that detached, instrumentalist relation to the world, a practice that integrates wild mind and wild earth.

This Ch'an integration of wild mind and wild earth grew naturally from dimensions of consciousness embedded at the deeper level of the Chinese language itself. There it functions as the very structure of thought and experience, a structure radically different from the dualism we saw in Western languages. Although we cannot change the fundamental nature of our language, we can understand the ways it structures our unthought assumptions by understanding how radically different classical Chinese is. And that understanding is liberating, for it reveals much about our original-nature and its inherent kinship with wild earth. In fact, the Paleolithic's remarkable survival into high Chinese culture is due in part to the very structures that make classical Chinese so fundamentally different from Western languages: its pictographic and self-less nature. In this, it is as close to the Paleolithic as written language could be.

There are many dimensions to the way classical Chinese renders wild mind integral to wild earth. Perhaps most important is the fact that classical Chinese is not alphabetic (cf. pp. 66–67). It is instead pictographic in its basic contours (the pictographic was augmented with phonetic elements), maintaining a direct and immediate relation between language and reality. The ideogram for "egrets," in the title of Tu Mu's poem, is 鷺, containing the graph for "birds" at the bottom: 鳥, which in its earlier form is 𩾌. And the poem itself is crowded with pictures of the ten thousand things, as a glance at the first line reveals:

| 雪 | 衣 | 雪 | 髮 | 青 | 玉 | 觜 |
|------|-------|------|------|-------|------|------|
| snow | robes | snow | hair | azure | jade | beak |

The ideogram for *snow* (雪) is a combination of *rain falling from heaven* (雨 in an earlier more pictographic form, or 𢁥 in the still earlier oracle-bone form) and *hand* (ヨ, stylized image of a wrist and fingers): hence, "rain you can brush away with your hand." Robes are clearly visible in early graphs as shoulders and sleeves above the ripple-and-sway of loose skirts: 衣). *Hair* is portrayed in two images of long flowing hair: the simple image at top right (彡), and a more complex one deriving from an oracle-bone image (𦥑) that later evolved into a stylized picture of hair so long that it must be tied with a band (—) and pinned with a hairpin (屮), as in this early form of the graph: 髟. 青, which refers to a range of blue-green colors found in nature, from forests to distant mountains, portrays a plant sprouting from the ground: 青. *Jade* depicts an ancient implement made of jade: 玉, from the oracle-bone 玉. And the main element of *beak* is

74

角, deriving from an original oracle-bone form meaning "horn" (𣥂) that evolved to portray an animal: 𧢲, showing a body with ribs that has horns on its head.

In addition, there is in classical Chinese no transcendental Self inscribed in the grammar (cf. pp. 67–68), as is immediately apparent when looking at this line from "Autumn Begins," a poem by Meng Hao-jan (689–740 C.E.) to which we will return later:

| 階 | 下 | 叢 | 莎 | 看 | 露 | 光 |
|------|-------|-------|------|-----|-----|----------|
| stairs | below | clump | grass | see | dew | radiance |

The first-person subject was rarely used in classical Chinese. In English, every time we say "I" it reinforces the bedrock assumption structuring consciousness: Self as a transcendental entity, an interior spirit-center separate from the exterior world (cf. pp. 67–68). That spirit-self therefore operates as an unnoticed assumption in our conceptual framework and in our everyday experience—quite aside from and prior to the Christian mythology of the "soul." In this line from "Autumn Begins," the perceptual verb *see* appears without the corresponding subject that a Western language would demand. Here, self exists as an absent presence in the grammar: we know it's there, but it isn't reified with a pronoun. And so, self-identity feels, at the foundational level of grammar, integral to the world.

The accuracy of this grammar (as opposed to the Western "I") is apparent in our everyday life if we look closely. As we have seen (p. 67), if we examine consciousness in the moment of perception, we find only empty-mind mirroring the world, containing it, becoming it. This is true of Meng Hao-jan "seeing" dew-lit bunchgrass. And it's why ancient Chinese poets often hiked among mountains: for there, on summits especially, perceptual experience can be so dramatic and captivating that it sweeps mind clean, empties it, leaving it nothing but mountain distances.

The same is true of thinking or feeling or remembering: if we examine what actually happens in consciousness during such activities, we can find no "I" there in the actual moment that they are happening. It is only our language and cultural assumptions that after the fact make us say "I" thought this or decided that, felt this or said that. In fact, when we look closely into the mental dimensions of actual experience, there is no "I" to be found as a discrete and enduring entity. Instead, if we try to locate that Self (mind/spirit-center) we take for granted in our routine activity, we find only the states and processes it supposedly directs. Whether gardening or cooking, talking or reading a book like this—if we examine closely, we can find no "I" directing the process, only the process itself. And so, that "I" is not noun, not something that exists somewhere inside us. It is verb: something that occurs through our interactions with the world around us: a weave of immersion. And this structure of consciousness is rendered in classical Chinese grammar.

Taken altogether, the nature of classical Chinese, especially poetry, creates an experience of consciousness in a boundless present, integral to earth's generative ontological process. In this, it embodies the insights of Taoist-Ch'an wisdom. As a matter of unthought assumption, consciousness is structured as a much more open and penetrating phenomenon than Western thought and language allow. This is consciousness woven through and through into the Cosmos, and it is our original wild-mind nature.

# 10

---

EARTH'S MYSTERIOUSLY generative nature must have been truly wondrous to primal people not only because of the unending miracle of new life seemingly appearing from nothing, but also because that miracle was so immediately vital to their well-being, providing them with food, water, clothing, shelter, and of course, a future in their children. Is it too much to imagine that as part of the Neolithic revolution, our transcendental spirit-center also grew out of an increasing awareness in males that they are fundamentally outside the essentially female nature of existence? That spirit/soul as an identity-center radically other than and outside of this material world: is it simply the structure of maleness? And was there an almost cellular anger and frustration caused by this profound sense of dislocation and irrelevance? Human violence toward the world is primarily male violence. Could this violence be in part the manifestation of that ongoing (but not consciously recognized) anger and frustration? And as women are earth's generative nature in human form, wouldn't that explain the history of seemingly inexplicable male violence against women?

It was apparently in the Neolithic when the Paleolithic's gynocentric worldview was replaced by an androcentric worldview: males compensating for their elemental irrelevance with androcentric ideologies and mythologies that put them at the center of things. Of course, there was a corresponding shift in social structure from gynocentric/egalitarian to androcentric male dominance—a shift in which women continued to be associated with earth by "spirit"-males, and treated with the same instrumental violence.[21] (Is it a coincidence that the West's new valuing of wild earth has coincided with a cultural shift in which women are again valued in a deep way?) In terms of the history we are tracing here, the grandest incarnation of this androcentric ideology is the Christian sky-god. Men conjured a male sky-god who in turn (is this a comedy?) created man in his own image (woman was a mere afterthought). Hence, the great and central mystery of creation was torn from the tissue of self-generative (female) existence and invested in some imaginal and male outside: a culture-defining mythological incarnation of metaphysical dualism.

Indeed, isn't metaphysics the ideational structure of a male outside in relation to a female/generative inside? And the male outside, the spirit-realm, was defined of course as the most true and real. From this, then, came the West's grand dualistic machine of metaphysics: inside and outside, subject and object, mind and body, human and nature, language and reality, spirit and matter, heaven and earth. We speak of humanity destroying the ecosystem, but in fact the male of the species has been the engine of devastation—not only in terms of male-dominated social structures, but even more fundamentally in "male" metaphysics—a detached and instrumental "outside" relationship to wild earth. And so, the Neolithic overthrow and suppression of the female (both socially and psychically) was an act of primal violence from which we may never recover.

––––––––––

In China, this male takeover was complete by the Shang Dynasty, with its male-dominated theocracy sanctioned and empowered by a male sky-god. The ancient Chinese were post-Neolithic, with a material culture shaped by separation from and control of "nature." Their everyday survival, like ours, was therefore dependent on an instrumental relationship to the earth. Even if classical Chinese avoids the problems of Western languages, people in ancient China not only had a written language, they were in fact intensely textual, with an extensive textual tradition. And in terms of social structures, theirs was a fiercely androcentric culture. The Paleolithic gynocentric survived across the centuries beneath that social surface, as the Taoist-Ch'an assumptions that shaped their "spiritual" experience. But ancient China's culture-builders did feel the wound of post-Paleolithic consciousness—kinship with the earth and its ten thousand things ruptured. Although that wound had no trace of the ontological/metaphysical breach that we know, there was a profound sense of displacement, even exile, and it fueled a powerful need to reconnect with wild earth at the deepest possible level, to reestablish wild mind kindred and integral to wild earth.

The earliest philosophical texts already considered this displacement to be the essential question of human self-cultivation, and Taoist-Ch'an spiritual practice centered on healing that wound of exile, replacing it with a sense of consciousness belonging to earth and its ten thousand things. It's a possibility that has been missing in the West, for there has been no female dimension: the Paleolithic is completely erased (as we have seen, when it was recovered at the beginning of the West's cultural transformation, it came from outside the Western mainstream, from lost ancient Rome and Native American indigenous cultures). But in China, spiritual practice always meant cultivating ways of reintegrating human consciousness with the generative tissue of existence. This began early with Taoism, which was later reformulated as Ch'an. In terms of ecological practice, Taoism-Ch'an centers on replacing the illusory spirit-center Self with consciousness integral to the broader world: a return to Paleolithic consciousness. And that practice is wholly applicable to our current situation.

Taoist-Ch'an understanding grew quite directly out of an oral wisdom-tradition extending back into proto-Chinese Paleolithic cultures, and it preserved much of the Paleolithic paradigm. Driving China's great cultural transformation, that paradigm survived into the earliest Chinese texts—*I Ching* (c. thirteenth century B.C.E.) and *Tao Te Ching* (c. sixth century B.C.E.)—originary Taoist texts constructed in large part from fragments of oral wisdom-literatures that were collected, translated, and compiled by editors into texts. The function of spiritual practice in the *Tao Te Ching* and later in Ch'an Buddhist teaching was essentially the same as in the Paleolithic: to cultivate consciousness integral to the vast and wondrous tissue of reality (Tao), to cultivate a sense of wholeness and belonging, a sense of home and kinship. Exactly what Jeffers proposed. And in the end, Taoist-Ch'an practice reveals one's truest self as the whole of existence-tissue Tao unfurling through its perennial transformations: again, a return to Paleolithic understanding.

Taoist-Ch'an practice cultivates this wild mind integral to wild earth at the level of immediate experience, as in fact the original-nature of consciousness. Indeed, Ch'an enlightenment was defined quite simply as "seeing original-nature": 見性 (*chien-hsing*, Japanese *kensho*). Ch'an grew out of the Taoism delineated by Lao Tzu's *Tao Te Ching*, which was apparently a resurgence of the Paleolithic that had survived beneath the surface of theocratic Shang Dynasty power structures. In this, it represents a return to the earliest levels of proto-Chinese culture, where the empirical Cosmos was recognized as female in its fundamental nature, as a magisterial and perpetually generative organism in constant transformation. In fact, Lao Tzu often refers to Tao as "female," "mother of all beneath heaven," etc. This is the root of a remarkable fact: high Chinese civilization, for all its complexity and sophistication, never forgot its origins in a gynocentric primitive. Indeed, it was the primitive that defined the distinctive nature of its complexity and sophistication. Here, spirituality is not a matter of belief and prayer as in the Shang Dynasty and traditional West, with their instrumental monotheisms—but of self-realization, which means healing that wound of consciousness torn from the generative tissue of things.

Toward this healing, Ch'an practice cultivates the original-nature of consciousness at its primal levels, prior to the illusory structures of self: wild mind as integral to wild earth, the tissue of reality and its ten thousand transformations. As we have seen, Ch'an practice begins with meditation, which reweaves consciousness and earth/Cosmos by emptying away the structures of self, leaving empty-mind mirroring the ten thousand things, thereby replacing self-identity with Tao's Great Transformation of things: the insight and, indeed, ethics of our egret poem. And so, again, meditation as perhaps our most fundamental ecological practice—as transformative ecological realization that is, at bottom, an embrace of the female.

Following White's logic, the eco-friendly Taoist-Ch'an conceptual framework should have produced a culture living in harmony with earth, like the Paleolithic. But the Chinese began early the wholesale devastation of their ecosystem, and there are a number of reasons for that. The culture was irremediably post-Neolithic and male-dominated. The masses were not shaped by the Taoist-Ch'an paradigm of the educated elite— instead, they were shaped by the metaphysical structures of myriad religious systems and remnants of Shang Dynasty monotheistic dualism. And finally, there was the sheer pressure of human survival needs. In the end, it was pure biology: the human animal, that apex predator, simply pursuing its own best interests, like any other animal. But perhaps most importantly: even with the ecocentric Buddhist ideal of *ahimsa* ("no harm") and the Taoist-Ch'an paradigm, the culture simply didn't have the technological capacity to provide full lives for the population without widespread environmental destruction.

The situation today is altogether different. We have the same basic social structure as ancient China, but we now have the ability to practice *ahimsa* and minimize ecological despoliation without sacrificing our quality of life. We have the ability to live rich lives in an environmentally sustainable, even celebratory, way. It is a great gift of modern science and technology, a true luxury. And there are many well-informed and insightful proposals describing how to do this: population reduction, carbon tax, clean energy, women's empowerment, vegetarianism, dismantling militaries, and on and on. What we lack, White and Leopold would say, is the conceptual framework (the "warp-threads") that would lead to this new way of life. It would need to be a framework commanding our "intellectual emphasis, loyalties, affections, and convictions," a framework operating not as debatable political advocacy, but as a bedrock assumption shaping human behavior—as the Greek-Christian paradigm has been, and the Paleolithic was before that. And it seems ancient China's Taoist-Ch'an framework offers just such a possibility.

# 11

---

To think about the world is to distance it. To analyze and understand the world is to possess and master it, and to devalue it as a detached object of our attention, stripping it of kinship. And that is our culture's whole relationship to the planet: analysis and understanding, which facilitates manipulation and exploitation. This understanding is necessary for survival (our dependence on the instrumental), but it is also fundamental to our destruction of planetary life. Meditation, on the other hand, replaces all that displacement with emptiness and silence: consciousness, therefore, without that instrumental and distancing thought. In this, it reveals the possibility of reorienting our relationship to earth in all aspects of our lives.

Perhaps more importantly, though, is how thoroughly humans live in an imaginal realm, and how that self-absorption cuts us off from immediate experience of the world around us (a self-absorption dramatically intensified by the virtual realm of television, computer, smartphone), for it precludes kinship as the texture of everyday experience. We can see it almost schematically in Wordsworth's 1798 poem "A Night-Piece," written at the beginning of the West's discovery of kinship with "nature" and in a voice that still dominates conventional nature writing and stewardship advocacy:

## A *Night-Piece*

———— The sky is overcast
With a continuous cloud of texture close,
Heavy and wan, all whitened by the Moon,
Which through that veil is indistinctly seen,
A dull contracted circle, yielding light
So feebly spread, that not a shadow falls,
Chequering the ground—from rock, plant, tree, or tower.
At length a pleasant instantaneous gleam
Startles the pensive traveler while he treads
His lonesome path, with unobserving eye
Bent earthwards; he looks up—the clouds are split
Asunder,—and above his head he sees
The clear Moon, and the glory of the heavens.
There, in a black-blue vault she sails along,
Followed by multitudes of stars, that, small
And sharp, and bright, along the dark abyss
Drive as she drives: how fast they wheel away,
Yet vanish not!—the wind is in the tree,
But they are silent;—still they roll along
Immeasurably distant; and the vault,
Built round by those white clouds, enormous clouds,
Still deepens its unfathomable depth.
At length the Vision closes; and the mind,
Not undisturbed by the delight it feels,
Which slowly settles into peaceful calm,
Is left to muse upon the solemn scene.

Here, a dramatic and unusual celestial event draws the "pensive traveler" Wordsworth outside himself: the moon breaks through cloud-cover, suddenly illuminating the sky, whereupon windblown clouds create the illusion that moon and stars are speeding across the sky, while at the same time remaining motionless. But this immediate experience, the actual world itself, is only the opening to what really matters here: a divine presence within the natural world. This presence is suggested by the religious feel of the language, the venerable tone and spiritualized vocabulary of Wordsworth's pantheism: "glory of the heavens," "vault," "dark abyss," "silent," "immeasurably distant," "unfathomable depth," and finally, the capitalized "Vision." And even after this Vision, Wordsworth's attention quickly turns inward again. Throughout, the spirit/matter dichotomy remains, this material realm valued only insofar as it reveals a spirit-realm. The self-involved walker remains radically separate from the scene—a spirit-center looking out on and contemplating an almost foreign realm.

In Meng Hao-jan's "Autumn Begins," the physical events are quite different from those in Wordsworth's poem, but the spiritual narrative is the same: inward preoccupation suddenly replaced by an intense awareness of the world. The same, and yet altogether different:

### Autumn Begins

Autumn begins unnoticed. Nights slowly lengthen,
and little by little, clear winds turn colder and colder,

summer's blaze giving way. My thatch hut grows still.
At the bottom stair, in bunchgrass, lit dew shimmers.

Like the Wordsworth poem with its "unobserving eye bent earthwards," "Autumn Begins" opens with Meng Hao-jan too preoccupied to notice the world. But it evolves very differently. What attracts Meng's notice is the beauty of an autumnal world dying into winter. His "thatch hut grows still," which is synony- ous with his mind going still—not because it is a metaphor for mind, but because empty mirror-mind occupies the same space as the thatch hut. From there, the poem moves to a con- clusion quite the opposite of Wordsworth's. "Autumn Begins" is essentially an act of meditation, and it ends with a perfectly empty mind mirroring a simple but striking empirical event: lit dew in bunchgrass shimmering. In the Taoist-Ch'an context, it is an enlightenment moment, when identity takes on its truest form: selfless and indistinguishable from earth's ten thousand wondrous things. This is an effect intensified by the fact that, as we saw earlier (p. 75), there is no "I" in the grammar, no "I" that "sees" the shimmering dew—a fact this translation struggles to represent, while losing the explicit presence in the Chinese of empty-mind mirroring the bunchgrass radiance. It's a cele- bration. And importantly, quite unlike Wordsworth's extraor- dinary and revelatory "Vision" of sailing moon and stars, this is an utterly ordinary moment. In this, it locates enlightenment (wholeness, belonging, healing) in the everyday realm where we actually live our lives.

Wordsworth's poem was written at the beginning of the West's great cultural transformation. "Autumn Begins," written almost eleven centuries earlier, embodies the understanding that the West's cultural transformation is only now beginning to reveal. In the poem, empty-mind knows the world with mirror- deep clarity, as the Cosmos open to itself. This reorients our relationship to the world, replacing separation with integration, alienation with kinship, isolation with togetherness—for in that mirror-deep awareness, the content of consciousness is quite literally the ten thousand things themselves. In Meng Hao-jan's simple glance out the door, consciousness and the expansive presence of existence are whole: wild mind integral to wild earth. And so, like "Egrets," "Autumn Begins" voices the culture's "intellectual emphasis, loyalties, affections, and convictions," its ethics.

"First Moon," written by Tu Fu (712–770) a few decades after "Autumn Begins," grows out of a meteorological event very similar to the one that interrupted Wordsworth's revery: the moon dramatically appearing for a moment, and then disappearing behind clouds. But as with "Autumn Begins," the difference between Tu Fu's Taoist-Ch'an kinship and Wordsworth's "worship of Nature" is foundational:

### First Moon

Thin slice of ascending light, radiant arc
tipped aside bellied dark—the first moon

appears and, barely risen beyond ancient
frontier passes, edges into clouds. Silver,

changeless, the Star River spreads across
mountains empty in their own cold. Lucent

frost dusts the courtyard, chrysanthemum
blossoms clotted there with swollen dark.

Like "Egrets," the whole poem operates in that mirror-deep enlightenment moment concluding "Autumn Begins"—for its statement is carried entirely by images rather than discursive statement, a landscape of images revelatory in their elemental thusness, rather than requiring some transcendental realm as in the Wordsworth poem. Indeed, this landscape of mirror-deep images is Tu's very identity in the poem, the very content of his consciousness. That cosmological landscape is the material out of which he constructs a complex state of mind that encompasses the entire universe, from the Star River (our Milky Way) to the chrysanthemums in his courtyard. It is, again, an act of meditation and a celebration of kinship.

# 12

THIS MIRROR-DEEP perceptual immediacy so fundamental to love and kinship was cultivated broadly by the ancient Chinese throughout their lives. They sipped wine as a way of easing self-consciousness, thereby clarifying awareness of the ten thousand things by dissolving the separation between inside and outside. They sipped tea as a way of heightening that awareness. And both of these practices ideally took place outdoors or in an architectural space that was a kind of eye-space, its open walls creating an interior emptiness that contained the exterior world around it—a physical incarnation of the empty mirror-mind opened by meditation, which they also practiced in such spaces.

The ancient Chinese cultivated wild-mind kinship in its most magisterial form when among rivers and mountains, where they aspired to dwell as integral to landscape. Cultivation of this dwelling took many forms, all of which recognized rivers-and-mountains landscape as the open door to realization. Rather than an expanse of physical terrain, they saw in the wild forms of mountain landscape the very workings of the Cosmos—

and immediate mirror-deep experience of mountain landscape opened consciousness most fully to the depths of those dimensions, to wild mind integral to wild earth. They found their spiritual home in mountains, thought of mountains as their teachers—and so, mountain landscape was the most natural site for their spiritual practices. They lived in cultivated reclusion among mountains as much as possible, where they also built monasteries. They practiced meditation among mountains, either alone at home or with companions in monasteries. Empty-minds mirror-deep, they wandered through river valleys and onto mountain summits. They dreamed mountains, and built their creative lives around them.

The arts cultivated rivers-and-mountains dwelling, arts which (as Leopold would recognize) helped the Taoist-Ch'an paradigm command the culture's "intellectual emphasis, loyalties, affections, and convictions," or as the ancient Chinese would put it: arts which were the "warp-threads" upon which their culture was woven. Indeed, the primary purpose of painting and poetry was to create artistic visions of rivers-and-mountains landscape. Such artistic practice was a way to *feel* our belonging to the existence-tissue Cosmos, as opposed to simply understanding it, a way to inhabit that rich belonging in everyday life, to celebrate it. In this, the arts were considered extensions of Taoist-Ch'an practice.

Calligraphers aspired to create with the selfless spontaneity of a natural force, evident most dramatically in the dynamic energy of their brushstrokes. Hence, calligraphy represents a deep ecological practice that opens the possibility of moving through life as something more than what we think we are, the possibility of moving the way rivers or weather or seasons move, free of that isolate and self-involved spirit-center. And that is to move as the Cosmos itself, which is nothing less than a return to Paleolithic consciousness. This is the wild mind that calligraphy enacts and renders visible, as the scroll on p. 94 reveals.

Painting was an extension of calligraphy, images built from calligraphy's dynamic brushstrokes. Painters crafted their artistic visions primarily from rivers-and-mountains landscape, infusing it with that dynamic energy: mountain landscape rendered as the most dramatic incarnation of Tao's living existence-tissue. These are landscapes that seem to subsume the viewer, rendered in a way that lets us enter into them and wander trails, explore canyons and valleys, streams and mountain peaks. This was the dominant strain in Chinese painting—quite unlike the West, where only late and briefly did painting open beyond the human realm (portrait, still-life, Christian iconography) to landscape. The wide world everywhere all around, boundlessly complex and beautiful and sustaining—and for over two thousand years, the West didn't consider it significant enough to enter the hallowed realm of art! Chinese rivers-and-mountains painting, on the other hand, renders the same vision as Paleolithic art: a breathtaking integration of human consciousness and landscape/Cosmos, which makes belonging to rivers-and-mountains not just an idea, but a wondrous and beautiful emotional experience (see p. 95).[22]

As we have seen in "Egrets" and "Autumn Begins" and "First Moon," China's poetic tradition follows the same rivers-and-mountains principles as its painting tradition, for the poems too enact belonging to existence-tissue landscape. And as with painting, comparison with the West is revealing—for, as we have begun to see, the differences could hardly be more extreme. Poetry was the dominant literary form until quite late in the Chinese tradition, and the poems we've seen are typical of its masterpieces: short and gentle poems that cultivate spiritual balance while attending to immediate and everyday experience,

Hsien-yü Shu (1257?–1302): *Song of the Stone Drums* (1301). Detail. Metropolitan Museum of Art, New York

丹臺春曉圖

天游為
伯顒畫

十年客邸絕塵蹤江上曉來思不窮
玉氣浮空春不雨丹光出井曉成雲
風前龍枕時堪倚月下鸞笙久
不閒章對仙翁遠孫子坐中觀畫
又論文

Lu Kuang (c. 1300–after 1371): *Spring Dawn over Elixir Terrace* (c. 1369). Metropolitan Museum of Art, New York

all with the purpose of integrating human and landscape. The West's epochal literary works, on the other hand, tend to be large constructions that consume the world within their human-centered visions—visions disconnected from landscape, earth, Cosmos, and inevitably dependent on Christianity's transcendental order. And those hegemonic forms are the vessel for storytelling that manifests the same human-centered assumptions.

The Christian Bible is of course Europe's great culture-building literature. A vast and human-centered imaginal realm, it proffers a creation myth giving humans dominion over earth, a foundational spirit/matter dualism, and a male sky-god establishing ultimate value outside our actual physical world. This is a god who thought nothing of visiting the Flood, a near-total mass-extinction event, upon the earth as retribution for human "sin"—a divine whim unconcerned with the wholesale destruction of wild earth and its countless individual creatures, not to mention humanity itself.

And the Bible's body of assumptions continues in the literary tradition shaped by its mythological scheme. When Dante finds himself in the "dark woods," he is utterly lost and despairing. Wild landscape like this was, of course, homeland for Paleolithic hunter-gatherers. And the ancient Chinese sought out wild landscape, felt that living amidst it was the richest and most civilized life possible. They built houses there with large windows that opened the landscape into their living space, and then surrounded those houses with gardens and terraces where they could sit among landscape, meditate, watch snowy egrets startle into flight and pear blossoms tumble away, write gentle wisps of poems. Dante, by contrast, embarks on a grand imaginal quest to escape those "dark woods," a quest in which the world is turned into an *Inferno* and *Purgatorio*, reality mined in an endless parade of metaphor and allegory as he pursues *Paradiso*:

a disembodied consummation in which woman (earth/body) is spiritualized into a form of God.

Milton's *Paradise Lost* is a massive biblical epic narrating an otherworldly battle between good and evil, God and Satan, in which this very world (the Garden of Eden) is mere stage-setting, and people (Adam and Eve) are little more than pawns. Even Wordsworth, who was among the earliest to value "nature"/landscape: his epic masterwork *The Prelude* is a sprawling poem that again subsumes landscape in its self-involved interests, for that landscape's function is as a beneficent influence that builds Wordsworth's soul. It's little different in his shorter lyrics, as we have seen. And in Herman Melville's *Moby-Dick*—which, like *The Prelude*, is directly engaged with wild nature—that wildness is again mined for metaphor and allegory: the white whale become a stand-in for the pantheistic divine, the mystery of existence, or the very universe itself. And of course, Ahab's obsession is to kill that magnificent being!

It's altogether different from the brief this-worldly utterances that are Chinese poems, or primal-culture tales that describe a community of human and animal and earth. Extending the Paleolithic, Chinese rivers-and-mountains poems manifest Taoist-Ch'an assumptions: the integration of human and landscape is the framework within which these poems breathe and speak. It is a vision of belonging and valuing earth's ten thousand wondrous things in and of themselves: wild mind integral to wild earth. There is an ethics in that, a complex of "intellectual emphasis, loyalties, affections, and convictions." And it's altogether different from the ethics and convictions embedded in Western literature's masterworks.

Yes, perhaps it's true nothing can save the planet at this point, perhaps the Sixth Extinction's Great Vanishing is already too far along. But if anything can, I suspect it's Tu Mu's vast little egret poem:

### Egrets

Robes of snow, crests of snow, and beaks of azure jade,
they fish in shadowy streams. Then startling away into

flight, they leave emerald mountains for lit distances.
Pear blossoms, a tree-full, tumble in the evening wind.

It's all too clear that the situation is dire, very likely irretrievable, and that placing so much hope in a little poem about egrets is no doubt wildly optimistic. But the simple fact that we can sense liberation in the incandescent clarity of this poem's gaze, feel the wonder and beauty of things occurring in and of themselves— that alone reveals how a paradigm shift is already far along here in the modern West, already moving us beyond those traditional human-centered assumptions that preclude our kindred love for this living planet and its ten thousand precious things. It reveals how that original Paleolithic mind is still very much alive within us. Those egrets leaving emerald mountains, pear blossoms tumbling: they may help us realize that we are much further along than we think, that all is perhaps not lost. And they may show us a way forward.

# II

## Wandering Boundless and Free

# 1

Before intention and choice, before ideas and understanding and everything we think we know about ourselves —we love this world around us. We are kindred, emotionally entangled. Ancient China's Taoist-Ch'an rivers-and-mountains practices represent the culmination of early China's great cultural transformation, and they could also complete the remarkably similar transformation underway here in the West. They cultivate empty-mind belonging to earth/Tao without any separation, which is love and kinship at the deepest level. And that reveals in immediate experience a broader philosophical principle central to Taoist-Ch'an thought and practice: that we are "unborn"—an understanding that appears to be one more way the Paleolithic experience of self integral to ecosystem survived into China's Taoist-Ch'an framework.

In that framework, death is a return home, a return to the generative tissue of Tao, to (as Lao Tzu says) the "nurturing mother," the "mother of all beneath heaven." And there was solace in that, belonging. But seen at a deeper level, we never leave home. Tao is all reality as a single living existence-tissue. The ten thousand things are not born out of it, never separate from it. They are always part of it. And it's the same for us—for mind and identity and every aspect of human civilization. It might seem that we are born out of Cosmos/Tao, that in death we return to it. But at these depths, however separate the center of identity may appear, with its thought and memory, we are each a fleeting form conjured in Tao's generative process of perpetual transformation: not just born out of wild earth/Cosmos/Tao and returned to it in death (which still assumes a center of identity detached from earth and its processes), but never out of it, totally *unborn* through and through, wild mind integral to wild earth.

This unborn kinship is our original-nature (the very thing Wordsworth and Thoreau and their compatriots yearned for and found in Native American cultures)—and yet, it all but vanished after the Paleolithic. It is difficult for us to inhabit that kinship, which is why spiritual practice existed in ancient China. Taoist-Ch'an cultivation of unborn original-nature is our most radical and deep ecological practice. But it is challenging. In ancient China, the great teachers were Taoist sages, poets and painters, Ch'an masters, rivers and mountains. We definitely need teachers like that, and thankfully they are still available to us. But our most elemental teacher may now be the Great Vanishing itself, earth's sixth mass-extinction revealing directly how kindred we are with wild earth through the emotional intensity of our planetary love and grief over the vast destruction and suffering and death.

Southern resident orcas slowly starving to death, so stressed that reproduction is rare, their population in steep decline: the Sixth Extinction teaching love. Vietnam's thirty national parks not actually wildlife preserves, but instead private hunting grounds where a genocidal campaign against primates supplies the rich with exotic meat (not unlike Italy's ongoing slaughter of songbirds for tasty morsels): the Sixth Extinction teaching kinship. Half the planet's animals already vanished, individual by individual, species by species, and much of the other half vanishing—red panda and California condor, vaquita porpoise and blue whale, Panamanian golden frog and hawksbill turtle, and even the bonobo and chimpanzee, our closest genetic relatives (sharing no less than 98.7% of DNA with us) vanishing, vanishing: all of it teaching love for this world, teaching kinship with its ten thousand precious things.

It's an emotional intensity that reveals our original-nature as wild mind kindred through and through with wild earth—and again, "seeing original-nature" is the very definition of awakening in Ch'an Buddhism. Awakening may seem difficult. Ch'an practices like meditation reawaken kinship, and we can still cultivate them—practices that unravel the Greek-Christian assumptions that structure consciousness for us, and so might stem the destruction. But what a strange blessing this teacher is, this unfolding eco-catastrophe: it reveals how easy it is, how we are always already awakened!

We have seen how, three millennia ago, the anthropocentric and spiritualized paradigm of Shang Dynasty China was transformed into the ecocentric Taoist-Ch'an paradigm. Then, it was the suffering inflicted by political tyranny that drove a wholesale transformation in consciousness. Here, after two centuries of teachers—from Wordsworth and Thoreau to Zen and Land Art—leading a slow transformation in Western assumptions, perhaps the Great Vanishing is itself our next teacher. With the suffering and death of mass-extinction already unimaginably vast, perhaps it is these grievous forces that will complete a similar transformation here—returning wild mind to wild earth.

We've seen much of what the Sixth Extinction's Great Vanishing has to teach us, all those insights of Paleolithic and Taoist-Ch'an understanding that have begun emerging here in the West. There's more, and we'll get to that. But for now, it's worth remembering that in denouncing the destruction of the planet, Robinson Jeffers was actually proposing a radical form of self-realization, a liberating self-transformation in which we reestablish our wild-mind kinship with wild earth and Cosmos. And the Great Vanishing is also revealing to us our most profound and beautiful and capacious selves. Calling forth all that love and joy and grief, it reveals our larger and more primordial self, our original wild-mind nature: again, the very definition of awakening in Ch'an Buddhism. And so, the Great Vanishing as an especially profound teacher in our age.

How strange that in cultivating this awakening, this wild mind integral to wild earth, we each cultivate not only our largest self, but also the possibility of ending today's Great Vanishing. How perfect that they are woven together: cultivating wild mind and cultivating wild earth! If we can't master what the Sixth Extinction is teaching, we will live with that vast wound of consciousness torn from existence. And at the same time, Jeffers's storm will continue arriving from "the long coast / Of the future to scour" our planet clean of the human. Indeed, in our kindred love of this world, it can be hard not to share Jeffers's feeling that, barring a wholesale transformation in human consciousness, the sooner that storm does its work, the better for wild earth as a whole.

# 2

LYNN WHITE's seemingly insightful and accurate thesis that a clutch of Christian ideas is the "historical root of our ecological crisis" is one among countless examples of how, even now in our modern scientific and secular world, we operate with the unnoticed assumption that we are spirit-centers radically separate from the world around us. We do this even if we know better, for it is unnoticed. White's proposition assumes ideas exist somehow in a realm of their own, detached from and contemplating the ten thousand things of empirical reality from a kind of outside spirit-realm. He assumes that they determine our behavior, that they somehow come first, and that if we could change to a more environmentally benign set of ideas, we could change our behavior.

There is clearly a lot of truth in that, and it offers hope, for sure. It allows us to imagine Paleolithic and Taoist-Ch'an paradigms offer rich and seemingly viable frameworks for building a more environmentally sustainable society. But we are in the end wholly *unborn* through and through. At the most foundational strata in the archaeology of mind, perception evolved through millions of years during which our human and prehuman ancestors navigated the world successfully. As they moved through the world, interacting with it, the world constantly honed perception to more and more accurately render the physical world. This was necessary for them to thrive and succeed. Our unthought perceptual understanding of depth and distance, solid and open, movement and shape, light and dark: they were all imprinted by physical reality into our ancestors' minds as the very structure of perception. Hardly the intentional action of a transcendental identity-center—the unthought assumption that gave rise to epistemology and much philosophical hand-wringing—perception is in fact consciousness woven inextricably from, indeed formed of and by, wild earth and its ten thousand things.

We have seen how, at the next strata up in the archaeology of our unborn mind, the seemingly transcendental Self is in fact constructed of the world around us—for mental states and processes are all built through metaphoric transfer from the stuff of empirical reality: from market scales to stars (p. 68). And isn't it the same for intelligence and its ideas—the next higher level in this archaeology of our unborn mind? Ideas, those strange contraptions through which we define self-identity and orient ourselves in the world: even in their grandest form as culture-defining (and ecosystem-destroying) ideological/mythological paradigms, ideas too are unborn. Indeed, we can trace *idea* back to the Greek *idein* and the Indo-European root *weid*, both meaning "to see" in the direct physical sense of seeing an object in the world. And so, *idea* not as a transcendental entity, but as the physical content of sight: a remnant of Paleolithic consciousness.

*Homo sapiens* speciated because we could adapt to rapidly changing conditions. We were scavengers, and that demanded inventive solutions to always new situations, leading to ever-increasing abilities of intelligence and imagination and creativity—the generators of ideas. As we expanded our range, we adapted to new environments all across the globe, many of which required entirely new sets of survival skills. And we invented whole new ways of existing—from scavenging to Paleolithic hunting and gathering, then on to Neolithic farming and modern industrial/capitalist/urban existence. The evolutionary adaptation that allowed us to do all this so successfully was intelligence. We were very smart, and that intelligence gave us the ability to adapt and exploit our environment effectively.

Intelligence is itself a clever adaptation that allowed the species to survive and thrive. It evolved in early humans to more and more accurately render and understand the physical world (the scientific process there at our origins!)—essential for survival as scavengers and hunter-gatherers. As with perception, the more accurate thought was, the more successful we were as individuals and as a species. And so, rather than a kind of transcendental realm looking out on the world, thought is a structure that world itself imprinted into our ancestors. The accuracy of thought is itself that imprint, is the world quite literally inside us, as us. And the more accurately those ancestors could not just *know* things, but also analyze their implications and imagine futures, the more successful they would be. Hence, our analytical and imaginative capacities are also the world imprinted with perfect accuracy inside us. And memory, that vessel where the identity-center seems most to reside, memory is no different. Human intelligence is *unborn*, not transcendental: it is the mysterious and wild world operating inside us. Indeed, this goes so deep that we cannot really think it, for it is the very structure of thought!

Reality dictates the shape intelligence takes, because it dictates what works. And that intelligence allowed us to spread across the globe and eventually dominate the ecosystem in an entirely unprecedented way. It allowed us to make more and more efficient tools, beginning with stone tools and continuing through to highway systems and computers. But of those tools, the most effective were no doubt the ideas and conceptual paradigms that govern our lives—and they too are simply evolutionary adaptations that dramatically increased our success as a species. Again, rather than existing in some transcendental sphere as White unsuspectingly assumes, ideas grow out of biology. They serve biology. That is, they are one more tool used by individuals, groups, and the species as a whole to impose their will on the world, to increase their evolutionary success.

The most powerful of those tools are the great cultural paradigms that govern our lives. And as White points out, the most potent of these was the Christian paradigm. In addition to mythologizing an instrumental and exploitative relation to earth, it tells (male) Christians that they are a chosen people carrying out God's design, that God is protecting and advancing their interest—and all that could only foster profound optimism and assurance and ruthlessness, which in turn engenders increased success. Paleolithic and Taoist-Ch'an frameworks seem to be accurate descriptions of reality, and more advantageous for the ecosystem as a whole, while the Western framework is clearly inaccurate and destructive. Nevertheless, the Greek-Christian framework became dominant simply because it is a more powerful tool for human evolutionary success.

If ideas and ideologies don't compete successfully in the evolutionary framework, they are superseded by more effective ideas. The mythologies of kinship with all life were effective in hunter-gatherer societies, preserving the healthy and balanced ecosystems that such societies needed to thrive over the long term, and they survived into Taoist-Ch'an refinements that operated in a cultural context very much like our own. But in the end, neither was able to compete with ideologies that put the human above and outside existence, ideologies that reify a spirit-center Self and enable an instrumentalist relation to the world, devaluing the non-human and making it available to unrestrained exploitation. Indeed, those cultural paradigms also dehumanized most of our own species, as well. "The other" provided a powerful selective advantage from the beginning. Tribes, races, nations, religions: by devaluing the other, they justified killing and displacing other people and therefore increased their own evolutionary success. We may see all this as tragedy, but the Cosmos's indifferent evolutionary perspective offers no judgment. Greek-Christian ideology simply works better as a survival strategy, like fangs or speed, and therefore European dominance spread, as did its destructiveness.

This has led to the crisis point we now face, a turning point where *Homo sapiens*'s cerebral survival strategies are beginning to fail. For like any other species that overstresses its habitat, *Homo sapiens* now faces its own decline and perhaps extinction. This is Jeffers's storm arriving from "the long coast / Of the future," and it is of course entirely *natural*. As both evolutionary theory and Taoist-Ch'an philosophy say: the one thing that never changes is change itself. And it is worth remembering that our closest relatives among the hominids thrived much longer than *Homo sapiens* has, but eventually went extinct. While *Homo sapiens* has been around for about 330,000 years, the proto-*Homo* primate *Australopithecus* survived something like 1.5 million years; *Homo habilis* thrived for a million years; *Homo erectus* 2 million years; and even *Homo neanderthalensis*, whose time on the planet we *Homo sapiens* apparently cut short, endured for 360,000 years.

# 3

IN THE END, then, it seems White is wrong. It isn't that immaterial spirits somehow came up with a bundle of bad ideas that then drove destructive behavior in the material realm. Seen from the Greek-Christian assumptions that White shares with our culture in general, assumptions underlying the current model of environmental stewardship, those "bad" ideas seem somehow unnatural, seem to come from that spirit-center operating in its own realm, a realm that even seems located essentially outside of earth's ecosystem. And it is enticing to think that if we could replace our self-involved and destructive conceptual framework with a more natural and caring relationship to earth, we might reverse the eco-disaster currently unfolding.

But mind and selfhood, thoughts and ideas like White's Christian paradigm: they are the ecosystem itself within us, and they grew out of the evolutionary process. They are wild earth operating inside us, as us. They provide the human animal the maximum amount of self-realization: pleasure, security, survival. Isn't this what any animal does, and isn't *Homo sapiens* just one more apex predator? The only difference is that we have a wild and apparently limitless passion to impose our will on the world, and fulfilling that seems for us tantamount to self-realization. Yes, a passion that is *wild* and completely part of our animal nature. And we have been stunningly successful in that wild passion, because a few anatomical quirks give us unique power to inflict vast devastation on the ecosystem. It is unlikely modern humans are happier or more self-realized than Paleolithic hunter-gatherers, especially at deeper levels where we now endure that wound of deracinated consciousness. The Greek-Christian paradigm has through science and technology and consumer capitalism (all perfectly unborn or "natural") transformed human existence in countless ways—some superficial and some genuinely good. And the human animal is unlikely to turn against its own self-realization, however poorly it may be conceived: there is little impulse to forego on principle things we think enlarge our lives: cars, bank accounts, medicine, airline travel, wine, astrophysics, children.

As we have seen, the transcendental Self is a powerful adaptation making the species more successful—for it separates us out, thereby allowing that powerful instrumental relation to the world around us. And again, it is wild earth that creates this spirit-center Self within us. We are woven through and through into the world. Thoughts, ideas—the structures of self-identity are not self-identity at all. They are quite literally wild earth operating "inside" us, part of wild earth as a single tissue unfurling through the sentient dimensions of the ecosystem: individual beings, all of which are interconnected, exactly as in the Paleolithic paradigm. It's breathtaking how we are at every level woven into the world. Far from our operating assumption that we are an inside directed at a world *out-there*, everything about us is always already that *out-there* itself. How boundless it feels—the very structures of mind, its every dimension, boundless with the intricate distances of wild earth!

We are unborn through and through, wild mind wholly integral to the generative existence-tissue of wild earth—and accepting this engenders a new understanding of our unfolding eco-catastrophe. We can now see the Sixth Extinction as a completely natural event: human depredation no different from past causes of mass-extinction: volcanos, asteroids, glaciers, methane eruptions, gamma-ray bursts. Because they occurred so long ago and did not directly impact us or the world we know, we can see those past extinction events as the Cosmos sees them, with that same indifference. We accept the massive species loss as simply part of the planet's inevitable and "natural" evolution. And from the unborn perspective, we can see today's mass-extinction event in the same way.

It's the way of things, appearing and flourishing and vanishing: animals, food webs, mountain ranges, continents, stars and galaxies, and also the diversity of earth's planetary ecosystems. Transformation always involves destruction, that vanishing of things that allows new configurations of existence to arise. It's even there in the moment-to-moment vanishing of thoughts and perceptions within consciousness, always opening space for new thoughts and perceptions. It's there in this book's flow of ideas—one idea after another, one sentence after another, each vanishing into the idea or sentence to come. And it's there in our familiar constellation of species diversity, now suffering a mass-extinction event that will open space for new constellations of diversity.

Earth's web of diversity is in a process of constant and endless transformation. It's the natural state of affairs, that web ceaselessly adjusting to variations in ecosystem conditions: always modulating climatic conditions, geologic change, species competition, etc. And in the history of life on earth, there have been many major extinction events, local and global, including five especially sudden and cataclysmic events in which the planetary constellation of diversity was drastically depleted, each time losing between 70 and 90 percent of species. We love this world, so it's difficult to see the current sixth mass-extinction as no different than the first five. It's difficult not to blame "unnatural" human ideas and activities for it, difficult not to think of humans as the great unnatural destroyer. And it feels like hard realism to admit, with Jeffers, that the sooner humans disappear the better for the whole. But today's Great Vanishing is no different than the earlier ones. Every aspect of human nature, the engine driving this extinction event, is just as elemental and natural and ineluctable as volcanos or asteroids or glaciers.

Although the difference in environmental impact of North America's native cultures and invading Europeans is almost total, it is still true that Native Americans were not immune to rapacious actions. And tens of thousands of years earlier in Europe, hadn't we already driven our sister species to extinction—the Neanderthals, with whom we shared passionate love and children, a species that actually survives in us, in our own DNA? Still more remarkable and even bizarre, seen from this broad planetary perspective, haven't we been at war even with ourselves, with the species *Homo sapiens* itself, forever and in so many ways? And even if everything has changed since the Paleolithic, nothing has really changed. Writing and alphabet and grammar, self and intelligence and idea, science and technology and capitalism, engines and factories, weapons and wars, power-generators and miles-wide drift-nets and our innate aggression and violence: it's all exactly like devastating volcanoes or asteroids.

After mass-extinction events, there is rapid re-speciation. The last mass-extinction event was the Cretaceous-Paleogene caused by an asteroid impact in Mexico's Yucatán Peninsula 66 million years ago (about a tenth of the 600-million-year span of life on the planet). It killed over 75 percent of earth's life-forms. But afterward, re-speciation was rapid and dramatic, conjuring this kindred world we love and crave even more profoundly than we can conceptualize. It conjured earth's entire aviary of birds: songbirds with their rainbow bursts of flight and song, snowy egrets leaving emerald mountains. And mammal speciation was especially spectacular, creating our most-loved companions: dogs and cats, horses, orca whales, primates. Creating us!

We love this world, this living planet, feel emotionally entangled with its ten thousand things. So it's no wonder that we cling to our familiar constellation of diversity. We choose some ideal moment to value absolutely and defend and lament, some moment before human destruction began in earnest—whether it's five hundred or five thousand or fifty thousand years ago. But another remarkable constellation of diversity was destroyed to make that moment possible. This fresh and exquisite world we inhabit is also aftermath, ruins, and its destruction can only open new possibilities that will likely be even more valuable and beautiful—for each mass-extinction leads to a more complex and remarkable array of diversity, because it begins with a more complex array.

Our moment is only one slice through a history of constant evolutionary transformation traversing hundreds of millions of years and including five mass-extinction events before our own. Here in North America, our moment is actually quite recent and short-lived: not just the web of diversity that emerged in the last 66 million years, but the web of diversity that recolonized North America after the last ice age, which was on the local scale an absolute mass-extinction event that ended only fifteen thousand years ago. (And part of that recolonization was the human migration onto this continent: again, the human animal as wholly integral to ecosystem.)

One slice through earth's ongoing natural history: we value this moment because it's the constellation of diversity in which we appeared and flourished, because our loving kinship entangles us in it. And we value this moment because it is the vast and complex web of beauty that we know and love, the ecosystem that supports our life. But we're only one among the countless species that appear and flourish and disappear in the ongoing evolution of life on planet Earth. Once we see from the unborn perspective, we can see this Sixth Extinction as a wholly natural outcome of cosmological evolution. And seen from that perspective, there is no reason to value our particular array of diversity above any other array, above whatever array will appear after this extinction event has run its course.

Perhaps the Sixth Extinction's most radical and profound teaching is that the Sixth Extinction is perfectly fine. This is to see with the utmost Taoist-Ch'an clarity, the clarity of a boundless Cosmos looking at itself, contemplating itself. In Taoist-Ch'an understanding, it might even be called enlightenment, transformational enlightenment in the face of the devastating reality of our age: existing wholly as your unborn self, your truest and most expansive identity that is the whole of Tao, ecosystem, wild earth, Cosmos. And in that awakening we move with the vast tranquility of the Cosmos—even now, as it unleashes this Great Vanishing. Tranquility, or even idleness—idleness, an ancient Chinese spiritual ideal of moving through everyday life with the same selfless spontaneity as the Cosmos. And we learn a bottomless kind of laughter at the sheer thusness of things unfurling from their inherent nature in the only way they possibly can. Laughter at how beautiful it all is—beautiful, even if terribly perplexing and disheartening.

Our truest self is the whole of this generative existence-tissue in perpetual transformation, is indeed whatever new possibilities this Great Vanishing opens. And wherever the Great Vanishing leads is equally beautiful. It's a difficult insight, but also ravishing. It's there in Tu Mu's egret poem. And it was there twenty-three hundred years ago, as Taoist-Ch'an understanding emerged at the end of China's great cultural transformation, when Chuang Tzu described enlightened sages living wholly in this unborn (deep-ecological) perspective:

for such people [birth and death] change nothing. All heaven and earth could be churned over and falling apart, but for them nothing would be lost. They inquire where nothing is false, and they aren't tossed about as things shift back and forth. They know the endless transformation of things follows its own inevitable nature, and they hold fast to the ancestral source ...

On loan from everything else, they'll soon be entrusted back to the one body. Forgetting liver and gallbladder, abandoning ears and eyes, they'll continue on again, tumbling and twirling through a blur of endings and beginnings ... wandering boundless and free through the selfless unfolding of things.[23]

# 4

THERE IS LIBERATION in that unborn enlightenment, liberation that opens us to our unbounded selves: wild mind unborn and integral to wild earth. It's a difficult liberation, carrying us beyond our human-centered assumptions, including our assumption that the human project is inherently good and even noble, that it justifies the ecological costs it exacts. And once those assumptions are left behind, we inhabit the indifferent perspective of the Cosmos. This is the Paleolithic and Taoist-Ch'an paradigm, the perspective proposed by Robinson Jeffers. It is absolute clarity. And yet. And yet.

Before intention and choice, before ideas and understanding and everything we think we know about ourselves—we love this world around us, this living planet. We crave it, hunger for it. Our tongues are hungry to taste and speak it. Our eyes to take it in. Our minds to contemplate it. Our bodies to touch it. How strange! As Jeffers and Taoist-Ch'an sages knew, the Cosmos is perfectly indifferent, and we are part of that indifference. But how wondrous: in us, the Cosmos somehow loves itself, loves the ten thousand things of this world, cherishes them! And so, paradoxical as it may sound, Chuang Tzu's seemingly heartless enlightenment also opens us to that elemental sense of love and kinship with this wide world all around us.

Infused with that love and kinship, Paleolithic hunter-gatherers lived with a profound and complex emotional world that is largely absent in us. Their lives depended on killing individual beings they recognized as kindred—as sisters or brothers; or ancestors; or most accurately, as past/future forms of themselves. And that could only elicit an intense feeling of grief for the killing and gratitude for the sacrifice that allowed their lives to continue, grief and reverent gratitude and a loving commitment to harm the least possible of that intensely kindred and precious world: *ahimsa*, Buddhism's loving nonviolence in which we avoid unnecessary harm. All of that infused with a celebration of belonging to a vast and mysterious tissue that extended far beyond their own existence, a celebration in which they relished the moment-to-moment beauty of it all.

This emotional complex was an ethics—an ethics that valued wild earth as home, as mother, as indeed our broadest and deepest self. And as we have seen, it is an ethics that values each of earth's inhabitants as kindred to and even indistinguishable from us, individual by individual by individual. At the foundational level where the ecosystem is a single tissue and we are each an unborn part of its whole, that existence-tissue is itself our largest and truest identity. That tissue's way forward is our own way forward, and the welfare of the ten thousand individual things is our own welfare. And so, until we value the ten thousand things, we don't value ourselves; and until we nurture them, we don't nurture ourselves. For if they don't thrive, we don't thrive; and if they don't survive, we don't survive. As we have seen, it is an ethics recognized early by Mencius, a contemporary of

Chuang Tzu: "The ten thousand things are all there in me. And there is no joy greater than looking within and finding myself faithful to them." And from that, it follows that only when we stop caring so exclusively about ourselves will we really begin taking care of ourselves.

In this profound sense of belonging as integral to the vast living Cosmos, we are the indifferent Cosmos not only mirroring and pondering itself—but also, feeling itself. Now, in the midst of this Great Vanishing, the Cosmos is learning in us a new version of that ancient Paleolithic emotional complex: an exhilarating sea-swell of heart-mind emotion. There's no word for it, this sharp amalgam of many feelings: joyful grief and gratitude, celebration and despair, reverence and anger, wonder and awe. And love. Again, the Cosmos is perfectly indifferent—and yet, how strange: through us it loves the ten thousand things of this world. And Ch'an practice returns us to that primordial love.

The Cosmos is pure mystery ceaselessly evolving in a process of transformation that is both rife with creation and ravaged with destruction. And yet, it is slow and steady in its processes, even tranquil. When we dwell as integral to earth and Cosmos, we inhabit our largest selves, our wholeness. Then, rather than clinging to a permanent self—a stable and enduring center of identity that sustains itself in turn by clinging to a constellation of assumptions and ideas and answers—we can share that tranquility, even as earth's process of transformation passes through the Great Vanishing of our contemporary mass-extinction event on its way to whatever new web of diversity may arise from it.

It is a tranquility suffused by that new emotion the Cosmos is learning in us: joyful grief and gratitude, celebration and despair, reverence and anger, wonder and awe and love, love and kinship—all of it tangled with the sense of radical wildness and freedom that comes of existing not as a circumscribed identity-center, but as woven into a dynamic and generative Cosmos. A wild freedom in which we move through everyday experience with the tranquility of the Cosmos, free even of death itself—for when death comes, whether our own or global mass-extinction, it comes as the existence-tissue simply unfurling its next possibility. From this emerges that bottomless laughter— bottomless because selfless, bottomless because there is no limit to wild earth's Great Transformation. Tranquility-infused wild-mind laughter at the mysterious unfurling of that existence-tissue.

This is how the vast wound of modern consciousness heals. In that healing, we resolve the paradox that only in embracing the Great Vanishing (including our own) as a perfectly natural part of planet Earth's evolutionary process, only then can we prevent the Great Vanishing. And if we can't do this, Jeffers's storm will continue gathering strength as it arrives from "the long coast / Of the future," scouring the planet clean of the human and so much else.

This is the paradigm Leopold and White couldn't quite see—a system of "intellectual emphasis, loyalties, affections, and convictions" that is not only ecocentric, but also accurate and breathtakingly beautiful, even liberating. It's a kind of flight, and that's how Chuang Tzu described it:

> If you mount the source of heaven and earth and the ten thousand changes, if you ride the six seasons of *ch'i* in their endless dispute—then you travel the inexhaustible, depending on nothing at all. Hence the saying: *The realized remain selfless. The sacred remain meritless. The enlightened remain nameless.*[24]

For us, it is wild flight in the midst of Jeffers's vast storm. And because the Great Transformation of things is inexhaustible, we are in this flight ourselves inexhaustible, inexhaustible in the radical freedom of wild earth's kindred beings all unfurling together through the Great Transformation—self gone, self replaced by the generative existence-tissue as a whole. Wild mind kindred and integral to wild earth: how mysterious and wondrous—it's an ethics! It's an ethics—this ecstatic freedom from all limits, this liberation in which we "wander boundless and free through the selfless unfolding of things!"

# 5

PERHAPS TODAY we are finding our way back to this primal dwelling. It proved to be a successful evolutionary strategy for tens of thousands of years in the Paleolithic, before it succumbed to the more successful strategy of metaphysical dualism, that detached "soul" armed with an instrumental relation to earth. However, the Paleolithic somehow survived as a guerrilla force beneath the surface of Shang Dynasty China and Greek-Christian Europe, cultures built on that wound of metaphysical dualism: consciousness torn from its kinship with wild earth. That Paleolithic dwelling became the Taoist-Ch'an paradigm that eventually migrated here to the West, where something remarkably similar has been reemerging independently over the last few centuries, begun in part during the age of the British Romantics by the Native American model of Paleolithic dwelling (p. 34 ff.). Now that the West's metaphysical dualism is failing as an evolutionary adaptation, this Paleolithic/Ch'an dwelling seems again to be our best survival strategy: wild mind unborn and integral to wild earth.

Our fullest identity, being unborn, is Tao itself—is all and none of wild earth's fleeting forms simultaneously. Taoist-Ch'an cultivation of original unborn nature is our most radical and deep ecological practice—and it is a practice cultivated in Tu Mu's little egret poem, where there is no identity-center separate from wild earth. It renders our unborn nature integrated wholly into landscape's mysterious unfurling. And it is, again, an ethics. When we inhabit our unborn nature, what we do to earth we do to ourselves. And from this, comes the ethical principle of *ahimsa*: the compassionate commitment to cause no unnecessary harm.

This understanding of our unborn nature seems more accurate to reality than our Western assumptions, for consciousness did in fact emerge from the evolutionary processes of this Cosmos. From cosmic dust came stars and planets, from planet Earth came increasingly complex life-forms, and from that increasing complexity came human consciousness. However unlikely it may seem from the Western perspective, we are each an opening of consciousness, an extraordinary opening in the opaque fabric of existence, a site where the Cosmos is aware of itself, where it mirrors itself in what can only be called a practice of elemental love. And more: we are each of us a new way for the existence-tissue Cosmos to see and know and feel itself, a new perspective. And that is true for all sentient beings, all higher animals with complex nervous systems. Perhaps that is the only thoroughly empirical ground for environmental ethics: the imperative to value each new perspective through which the Cosmos sees/knows/feels itself.

It's another way of understanding the basis of Buddhism's *ahimsa* ethics. Ch'an calls that opening of consciousness our Buddha-nature. It says all sentient life possesses Buddha-nature. And in sharing this Buddha-nature, each sentient being is also

Buddha, is also a singular and profound and beautiful opening of consciousness. Indeed, those sentient beings were considered sage teachers in ancient China. They have no need of Ch'an spiritual practice, for they are always already awakened. That mirrored opening is the nature of their everyday experience. In this, animals reveal to us our most primal nature, that inner wilds where we are kindred to egrets, where we too are the awakened landscape gazing out at itself. And rivers and mountains too are Buddhas revealing in their elemental silence our original empty-mind nature. So, animals and rivers-and-mountains landscapes both carried the utmost ethical value, not just as our equals but indeed as our sage teachers. To harm or kill them is therefore to harm or kill our most profound teachers—or indeed, the very Buddha that we all are.

It's not as simple and direct now as it was for Paleolithic hunter-gatherers, not a direct individual relation to other individuals in the community of life. This ethical framework needs to be applied through our complex relation with earth, abstract and indirect, where our actions have distant and unseen impacts— hence, a framework of legal and regulatory and educational principles governing our ethical relation to wild earth and its ten thousand things. But it seems possible, tantalizingly possible, that we might succeed in changing our paradigm, changing our alien identity-center to a sense of belonging wholly to earth's processes. As we have seen, there is a rich precedent in ancient China's cultural transformation. And "existence precedes essence," as Sartre said: rather than being defined by some predetermined and ineluctable human nature constructed by the Western tradition, we are free to define anew our nature and our future at any moment. It doesn't seem difficult to imagine our technology deployed according to assumptions of human belonging and ecological responsibility, radically mitigating the ongoing eco-catastrophe while also providing us with satisfying lives. Indeed, our technological prowess theoretically makes possible lives less destructive than in the Paleolithic—for killing large numbers of kindred creatures is no longer necessary for survival.

In fact, after the great transformation in Western assumptions that has blossomed over the last two centuries in the West, isn't that new ecocentric paradigm already becoming reality? Even if our culture is still very much under the sway of Christian mythology, aren't we realizing more and more every day, in a steady stream of research and books, how the interior lives of individual animals like those orcas are so similar to ours: rich in emotion and dream and understanding, culture and social connection? That's important, a beginning, though it takes our own interior lives as the standard by which others are valued, which is another form of our human-centered perspective. For such a claim fails to value animals in and of themselves and on their own terms. In any case, that paradigm shift is simply a recognition of the "original-nature" always there in us, that Paleolithic kinship with wild earth. Don't we feel love and empathy and kindredness with the non-human? Don't we feel joy when we see an animal thriving or joyful (that mother orca eventually reappeared and several years later gave birth to another baby that has so far thrived!), and grief when we see an animal suffering or dying? Isn't there a vast grief haunting us as we face the dying of our entire planetary ecosystem? And isn't a large portion of the human race now advocating defense of the earth? Here in America, to take one particularly noteworthy example, there is a sprawling system of wilderness areas—and however token they may seem, they function as public declarations defending the intrinsic value of wild earth itself, of its own self-realization completely outside our human interests.

We concern ourselves with species, local and planetary eco-systems. But that is one more version of our human-centered approach. Species and ecosystems are abstractions arising from our human perspective, and they are inevitably valued in terms of what they provide for us. But species and ecosystems mean nothing at all to the sentient beings involved. For them, all that matters is their own individual lives, their own families and communities, their own habitats. In our Western framework, even in the contemporary stewardship model, those individuals are still considered qualitatively less valuable than humans. We may be concerned with whole species—the tragedy in our minds of an entire species vanishing, the frightening finality of that. But we rarely concern ourselves with individuals themselves, which leaves the field wide open to the kind of compromise that has made environmental policy so inadequate. But in the Paleolithic and Taoist-Ch'an paradigms, each individual animal is kindred and precious, its own self-realization no less important than our own. Indeed, it participates in our own selfhood. And so, its self-realization is valued as our own.

We are so much more than what we think we are: empty-mind, unborn mind, wild mind. And there was no fundamental distinction in ancient China between mind and heart: 心 connotes all that we think of in the two concepts together. In fact, that ideogram for "heart-mind" is a stylized version of the earlier 心, which is an image of the heart muscle, with its chambers at the locus of veins and arteries. Empty-mind and mirror-mind, unborn mind and wild mind: it is all equivalent to a full heart. Fundamentally then, Ch'an opens us to love's most profound dimensions, that kinship in which we are emotionally entangled through and through with the world: wild mind integral to wild earth. Here, ethics involves individual acting in relation to individual, both integral to earth and both equally valuable.

Hence, acting from a responsibility to other individuals. It's an ethics revealed directly when we see with the "inhuman" (Jeffers's word) clarity of the Cosmos, which is to see as a mirror in which the world comes alive as it is in and of itself—in all its thusness, beautiful and mysterious, and intrinsically valuable individual by individual by individual. And it's the ethics celebrated in Tu Mu's vast little egret poem, with its empty-mind mirroring:

### Egrets

Robes of snow, crests of snow, and beaks of azure jade,
they fish in shadowy streams. Then startling away into

flight, they leave emerald mountains for lit distances.
Pear blossoms, a tree-full, tumble in the evening wind.

What is the relation of egrets and pear blossoms? What is the logic of the poem's leap from egrets rising to pear blossoms falling and scattering away? Isn't it pure mystery, a particularly beautiful and resonant kind of mystery, as they echo each other: white egrets lifting away, their forms fluttering with wingbeats; white pear blossoms tumbling downward, their petals fluttering the same way? And what's left afterward but the mysterious emerald mountains themselves: still distances, sage silence whispering in the wind.

To see with the mirror-deep clarity of the Cosmos seeing itself—that is to inhabit in immediate experience our original unborn nature, to give ourselves to this wild mystery and wonder. There, we are ourselves indistinguishable from mountains and egrets and pear blossoms, are therefore also scattering away through the Great Transformation. In this, we know our unborn belonging to the tissue of existence: its ten thousand things in their vast transformations. And so, an unborn and primordial ethics: what a wild heart does to wild earth, it does to itself.

Wild earth tends toward balance. Anytime and anywhere it slips out of balance, there is a response mechanism that establishes a new balance. This is a constant process always in play over many dimensions. To take one simple but relevant example: when a predator's population grows too large, prey become scarce, and soon the predator population declines to a new balance point. At the moment, human population and activity has grown much too large, far out of balance, placing remarkable stress on the planet's ecosystem. The Sixth Extinction is teaching us all about our elemental kinship with the ten thousand things, returning us to our original-nature as wild mind and wild heart, to our wild love for this world and the unborn and primordial ethics it engenders. Perhaps this is earth trying to compensate and reestablish balance. We shall see if it works, or if Jeffers's devastating storm will continue sweeping over us and other balancing mechanisms come into play, issuing forth who knows what strange and kindred new mysteries wandering boundless and free through the selfless unfolding of things.

# Notes

1. *Existentialism Is a Humanism* (1946), p. 20 and *passim*.
2. "Ancient Chinese" refers throughout this book to the educated elite, the artist-intellectuals who ran the government and built high Chinese culture (philosophy, poetry, painting, etc.), not the uneducated masses whose allegiances were to myriad religious belief-systems.
3. Letter to Sister Mary James Power (Oct. 1, 1934). In *The Wild God of the World: An Anthology of Robinson Jeffers*, p. 189.
4. "The Answer." Jeffers's poems appear in many selected and collected editions, including two recent examples: *Rock and Hawk* and *The Wild God of the World*. The poems cited in these pages can generally be found in any of those editions.
5. "Carmel Point."
6. *Mencius* XIII.4. See my *Mencius*. Also in my *The Four Chinese Classics*.
7. Preface to *The Double Axe & Other Poems* (1977), p. xxi.
8. "November Surf."
9. *Science* 155, 1967. White's essay has been widely anthologized, and it has generated an industry of writing in response to its ideas.
10. *Of Plimoth Plantation*, journal entry for Sept. 6, 1620.
11. See David Graeber and David Wengrow's *The Dawn of Everything* for the transformational influence of this "indigenous critique" on European culture. And for the impact of Native American culture on the Romantic poets, see Tim Fulford's *Romantic Indians: Native Americans, British Literature, and Transatlantic Culture 1756–1830*.

12. *The Prelude* (1805), Book I, lines 294–307.

13. See especially Humboldt's *Cosmos* (German publication 1845, with English soon after), which contains all the quotes that follow. For a guide to Humboldt and his influence, see Andrea Wulf's *The Invention of Nature: Alexander von Humboldt's New World* (2015).

14. "Vorticism" (1914).

15. *Paterson* (first draft, 1926; published 1946–58) *passim*.

16. Both quotes from Olson's seminal essay "Projective Verse" (1950). Olson's other seminal essay for this line of thinking is "Human Universe" (1951).

17. This tradition is traced in my *The Wilds of Poetry: Adventures in Mind and Landscape*.

18. "Hurt Hawks."

19. "The Wilderness" in *Turtle Island* (1974).

20. In *Language, Thought and Reality* (1956). Whorf's essay has been widely anthologized, and it has generated an industry of largely critical response. But it has weathered the criticism and remains compelling in many ways.

21. This history is evoked in Susan Griffin's *Woman and Nature: The Roaring within Her* (1978), an important contribution to America's postwar cultural revolution.

22. For a full account of these philosophical dimensions in Chinese painting, see my *Existence: A Story*.

23. Chuang Tzu 5.1. See my *Chuang Tzu: The Inner Chapters*. Also in my *The Four Chinese Classics*.

24. Chuang Tzu 1.10.

# Acknowledgments

"Autumn Begins" by Meng Hao-jan, translated by David Hinton, from *The Mountain Poems of Meng Hao-Jan*, copyright © 2004 by David Hinton. Reprinted by permission of Archipelago Books.

"Egrets" by Tu Mu, translated by David Hinton, from *Mountain Home: The Wilderness Poetry of Ancient China*, copyright © 2002, 2005 by David Hinton. Reprinted by permission of New Directions Publishing Corp.

"First Moon" by Tu Fu, translated by David Hinton, from *The Selected Poems of Tu Fu*, copyright © 1989, 2020 by David Hinton. Reprinted by permission of New Directions Publishing Corp.

"The Lights in the Sky Are Stars" by Kenneth Rexroth, from *In Defense of the Earth*, copyright © 1956 by New Directions Publishing Corp. Reprinted by permission of New Directions Publishing Corp.

"Wave" by Gary Snyder, from *Regarding Wave*, copyright © 1970 by Gary Snyder. Reprinted by permission of New Directions Publishing Corp.

*Phil Dera*

DAVID HINTON has published numerous books of poetry and essays, and many translations of ancient Chinese poetry and philosophy—all informed by an abiding interest in deep ecological thinking. This widely acclaimed work has earned Hinton a Guggenheim Fellowship, numerous fellowships from NEA and NEH, and both of the major awards given for poetry translation in the United States: the Landon Translation Award (Academy of American Poets) and the PEN American Translation Award. Most recently, Hinton received a lifetime achievement award from the American Academy of Arts and Letters.